The Roadmap to an
Enriched Life

The Roadmap to an Enriched Life

Harold Deonarine

iUniverse, Inc.
Bloomington

The Roadmap to an Enriched Life

iUniverse books may be ordered through booksellers or by contacting:

iUniverse
1663 Liberty Drive
Bloomington, IN 47403
www.iuniverse.com
1-800-Authors (1-800-288-4677)

ISBN: 978-1-4620-8387-9 (sc)
ISBN: 978-1-4620-8389-3 (hc)
ISBN: 978-1-4620-8388-6 (ebk)

Printed in the United States of America

iUniverse rev. date: 01/05/2012

CONTENTS

Dedication

To my parents, for the knowledge and good values they instilled in me as a young man growing up in Couva. They have showed me the path of love and kindness and an unending supply of support.

To my two beautiful children Anandi and Aditi who believed in me and let me know that I am the best dad.

To my wife Arti, for putting up with me over the years and keeping me in line.

To our pets at home Papa and Lil Mama, the two best cats in the whole world who wait up for me every night.

Book Comments:

(1.) "This friendly guided journey to achieving your own personal success is to the point and inspiring. Harold pulls you in and takes you step by step through the process of finding and achieving your life's passion."

"A comprehensive, thought provoking push to get you into action working towards your dreams."

Isik Kayhan, CEO,
Bio Focus

(2.) The contents of his writing touches one right at the heart. His narration of the sequence of events is well chosen and presented. His explanation and analysis to present an idea is clearly impartial. In short very inspirational, emotional, impactful and motivational journey that he took us through.

Lincoln d'Souza,
Manager,
Rochestor Midland

FOREWORD

Life is clearly anything but simple, in fact it is probably all of the trials and tribulations of life that direct us, confuse us and ultimately, define us. However, if we can take from life's experiences, both good and bad, some basic and fundamental guiding principles and practical theories, then maybe, just maybe, we can carve out a road less travelled for ourselves, defy the general idea that fate dictates our outcome from birth, and develop superior personal behaviors to guide us all to greatness, in both our personal and professional endeavors. Just maybe, with a little help from a friend?

I would assert to you all that within the walls of this text, written by a personal friend and colleague of mine, you will not only be able to relate, on a very personal level, to the stories and examples therein, but you will also be able to put into ACTION, through a very intimate individual journey of change and empowerment, key strategies for the improvement and betterment of your life, as you know it right now.

The true "magic" behind _The Roadmap to an Enriched Life_, lies in the simplicity of its knowledge, the author's passionate discourse and the absolute TRUTH of its counsel. I am confident that there is not one average person out there who could not understand, embrace and emulate the ideas within it to immediately see an IMPACT on the quality of their personal existence.

Once you read this "lifestyle treasure manual" (as I have come to call it), I'm sure that you will share with me a deep understanding of Harold the man . . . his courage, his drive for fulfillment, his passion for authenticity, and his deep desire to compassionately share with others his successful strategies, and more particularly, for taking YOUR LIFE in a NEW and exciting direction. Your choices, your direction, your passions and ultimately your own path to true HAPPINESS, every single day, for the rest of your life.

Let's not wait even one more minute and please listen very carefully . . . without further ado, I give to you, without hesitation, my friend and now yours . . . Harold.

Rob Gonsalves
VP Operations

"The Secret and the Magical mind is within you; use it wisely and a world of possibilities exists."

~ Harold

All over the world, people sit and ask themselves: "Where is the road to a fulfilling life?" A very fortunate few stumble upon the answer early on. Some people realize it later on; some regret not having it soon enough for success; and some go without finding the answer. My book is not the answer to your problem. Oh, no. It is not the magic potion to your maladies and not the cure for your riddled mind. This, my dear friends, is simply a way for me to help you find the answers; to go deep within and explore your mind power. I will be discussing the very basics of fulfillment, and hopefully how to attain it with the aid of your individual prowess.

Friends, from my experience, there is no communal experience in terms of having a life well-lived. It is, to me, always a question of individuality; always a question of how you perceive it. For most of us, it is measured by how much you earn; your net worth. To some people, it may simply be the ability to help and see the look of satisfaction in the eyes of others. And to others, it may be as simple as a cup of coffee on a cold, rainy day.

As you can see, a fulfilled life is different from each individual's perspective. It is never constant in terms of standards. What is common among the various perspectives is that it is always the attainment of a particular goal. In this sense, the harsh realities of life will always have stuff to throw at you, and it is for this particular reason that I am writing *The Roadmap to an Enriched Life*. This is a guide from my perspective. I hope that it may help you strengthen and enrich your perception, or even help you discover your own viewpoint.

In this book, I will be presenting tips and methods through which the feeling of contentment from living your life well may be attained, as well as stories to help you relate to the humanity behind the methods. I hope that I may be of help to you as you read through this book.

Although you may not turn out to be a 'fulfillment Houdini,' I am sure that you will have some idea as to how it works.

Ladies and gentlemen, welcome to the little world that I would like to call 'Perspective.'

PART 1

SUCCESS

CHAPTER 1

AN OVERVIEW

"We will often find compensation if we think more of what life has given us and less about what life has taken away."

–William Barclay

I believe that success is never determined by intellect, riches or influence. It is my firm belief that success is more than just a destination; it is a journey as well. Most of us look up to the stars, hoping for one of them to fall so that we can make a wish, or close our eyes to wish before blowing out the candle. We dream of seeing that star and we feel kind of giddy after blowing out the candle, because it somehow gives us hope that in one way or another we can say that our wishes may come true. And in those cases, most of us wish for success. Talking about shooting stars and birthday candles, I believe that people have to break free from living their lives based on what others would call The Fates. If we wish to become successful in life, then we must do more than just wait for stars to fall or birthday candles to be lit. We must, in all aspects, strive to be successful.

Many consider success to be elusive, but in nature it is not. It has no feet, no arms and no means to travel around. It is not something that people need to chase, but something that may be chasing you and you cannot recognize it. Success is never a smooth ride, and success is not a state of being. Success is a state of mind. The only thing that we have to remember is that the world will always have its standards, and that success will only be elusive if we look at it from the world's point of view. We need to remember that the only person we need to convince is ourselves, and that it is our standards that we need to meet in terms of success.

The nature of the word *success* is very broad, and one may arrive at various conclusions if success is considered within different contexts. Some view success as being able to earn their first million by the age of 40; others view success as managing to earn a living and being able to provide for their families. Some view success as being able to drive their own car and others as learning to ride a bicycle. There are people for whom success is preparing a sumptuous meal for an evening of merrymaking; and for some, success means finding something in the dumpster that will serve as a decent meal for the day. You see, success is not supposed to be viewed from a singular perspective or measured by one standard. Success should be viewed according to individual standards—for it is you who needs to achieve it.

Our successes are not determiners of the absence of failures. It is, beyond a shadow of a doubt, a result of learning from our failures. It is not how much has been taken from us, but how much we are left with, and how we manage to get up and dust ourselves and move on. My friends SUCCEED!

Numerous books have been written to address the mystery that is success. But what is so mysterious about it? Is it the definition that embodies it? Is it the process by which it is achieved? Or is it simply its nature that we cannot fathom? Success, as they say, starts with a state of mind. Success begins with a thought.

Plant a seed. Take care of it, nurture it and watch it grow. The seed becomes a plant, and that plant will multiply many times over.

Let me start by telling you a true story:

This story comes from Milton, Ontario, Canada. It is about a young man who many years ago had a dream and hope of planting a shorter variety of apple trees and a better orchard than could be found in Ontario; a place where families could bring their children to pick apples and have a fun-filled day. The odds were stacked against this man because there were no plants that were short enough to enable the fruits to be picked without the use of a ladder. But this ambitious young man did not listen to the naysayers who told him that such apple trees did not exist. This young man persevered and eventually found someone located in England, and a new variety of apple trees were born.

Have you heard about the Chudleighs? They are the farmers with the biggest apple orchards in Milton, Ontario. The Chudleighs were the first generation of farmers that had such a dream and, after many continuous uphill battles for survival; they are today, the premium apple growers in Ontario. Today, they own hundreds of acres of apple orchards across the province with a large manufacturing facility that produces one of the finest apple pies in the world.

Now, start taking notes, because this story is worth its weight in gold. Sadly the young man and his wife died tragically in a car accident. Tom, the man's son, and his wife Carol took over the apple farm and along with their three sons, they worked in the farm from early morning to late at night, on a daily basis. They were simple, good people with little money, and Tom, Carol and their boys wanted to continue the magnificent dream. It was not smooth sailing from that point but things got worse. At one point the farm burnt down, and with little money and nearly bankrupt, they decided that they must do whatever it takes to keep the farm. So, using an old little pickup truck, they went from door to door, marketing and selling their apple pies, by the slices and whole pies, in the neighbourhood. They even gave away a lot of samples so that people could get a taste of the wonderful delicious pie. Following a huge uphill struggle fraught with problems, they eventually made a breakthrough. The business grew, because people loved the pies. The farm became a success and families brought their children to the farm. Dean and Scott recognized the potential of the farm, attended university, worked hard and today they are the premium pie and dessert makers in Canada. They export most of the products to countries around the world and are a phenomenal success.

You see, my friends, when you are seeking success, do not give up when the curve ball is thrown to you. That curve ball is meant to twist you into looking at another direction. Never up on your dreams as the universe works with you in strange ways to help you get there.

When I interviewed Dean, the CEO of the company, I asked him what piece of advice he would give to people. He said, "Harold, my advice is to go after your passion, create a list of things you wish to accomplish, set a date and do it."

Remember that if you love what you do, then pursue it with passion and success will follow. I would like to begin discussing success by starting from a simple premise: The formulation of a vision.

STEP 1

THE VISION OF SUCCESS

Success is a thought process first, followed by perseverance and hard work. As the saying goes, "The journey of a thousand miles begins with a single step." I believe that there is no other fitting analogy for success than that of a journey. So, where does success begin? It begins with that single step or, in this case, a single thought.

Many people say that it's all in the mind. I say that it *starts* in the mind. For one person to be successful, he or she has to first envision that success. It acts like a goal, which that particular individual has to achieve and when you have a goal, you have something to strive for. Reason and purpose fuel our endeavours. Without reason or purpose we simply refuse to act because it is of no significance.

So, the first thing that you have to do is to picture yourself as successful. Call it weird if you wish, but sometimes even daydreaming helps. The things you envision when you daydream, that beautiful sports car, that job you have been eyeing, that wonderful house by the lake; these are all successes waiting to be attained. When people consider these things as merely dreams, or even nature's turndowns, I believe that this is when people stop being successful. When you give up on your dream, you no longer exert effort to achieve it and it is this that makes people unsuccessful.

Imagine a shiny, brand new sports car. Let's say it's a Ferrari or a Lamborghini. Then, let's imagine a rundown, beaten car. Let's say, a Ford Pinto. The Ferrari and the Lamborghini are fancy to the eyes; real beauties, if you ask me. The Pinto, on the other hand, is a wreck. Yet no matter how fancy or rundown these cars may be, they still would not run without gasoline. Your mind is your energy source. Tap into it and you will see the power of the mind. This is what keeps the body active.

You may have big dreams and you may have small dreams. But if you do not gas up, you will never be able to start that car and zoom away.

About 26 years ago, back in Trinidad, my wife, unbeknownst to me had written on a piece of paper that she would be living in Canada by a certain date. She visualized it, and years later we ended up immigrating to Toronto, Canada. If you can visualize things with clarity in your mind, the subconscious mind has no alternative but to comply with the instruction. Be creative, visualize with great clarity, repeat it and that dream becomes a reality. The body gets energized to force you to go after your vision. Give it a set date and find a way to accomplish this goal, vision or dream, and before you know it, time will have passed by and your dream will have been fulfilled. You *must* work on your dreams.

When I left Trinidad so many years ago, little did I know about the power of thought, but I knew I wanted a better and safer life for my girls; I wanted them to be independent and happy. Today, both girls have completed university, travelled the world, and are well accomplished. That part of my dream has been fulfilled. Today, my next vision is that someone somewhere will read my book and find something that they can relate to their life, and that it will make a difference.

Do you see the picture now, friends? There is power in that thought; there is might even in daydreams. Most of us would say that we all have to wake up from these dreams. I say differently. I say, "Wake up and act upon those dreams." My suggestion is: Do something, do anything, just give it a try. Gas up, my friends, and start your journey towards success!

STEP 2

MAKE A SHOPPING LIST

Many of you may ask me what a shopping list has to do with success. Apart from it being very therapeutic, I believe that it *has* something to do with success. Why is it a step towards success? When talking about shopping lists and success, I do not mean it literally. What I mean is something related to a shopping list, and that which performs the same function.

Have you watched the movie *The Bucket List*? In that movie the characters made a list of the things they wanted to do before they die. Most of these dreams were radical, and some were simple dreams. And they made it a point that they will have achieved everything on the list.

What I am proposing is that you write down things that you want to achieve. And no, this will not be your "bucket list". This will serve as your checklist for success. Before you go "shopping", I suggest that you indicate the things you want to achieve in your life and try to group them according to the duration by which these dreams are to be achieved.

Let me give you an example.

My Shopping List

- Go Sky Diving
- Enrol in an MBA program

- Become a motivational speaker
- Complete a 42k marathon
- Own a Range Rover Sport
- Do CN Tower Edge Walk
- Build a second house near the lake
- Retire
- Travel around the world

Some pointers are worth noting, because *The Roadmap To An Enriched Life* is written with the intent to make an impact in your life; it is written in with simplicity so that it becomes an easy read. Let me start by giving you some ideas to plan your life.

1. Decide where you are in your life. Be very honest about your life situation and decide what you would like to become should the opportunity arise.

2. Now, make a plan as to the period of time in which you would like to achieve your plan.

3. Surround yourself with people who can mentor you, and whom you can mentor as well.

4. Have courage and say to yourself, "I will make this possible. I will work for it. I will trade time for my dream, I will never give up."

5. Speak to anyone who may be able to assist you, but be prepared for a lot of rejections. To get where you want to go is a journey that only you must travel. It is going to be a lonely, long road. Give it time; as it takes time to make things happen, so give it a reasonable period during which you are sure you are willing to commit. If you do not do this, you will become frustrated and give up.

6. If you are quite sure that it will cost some time, then make a plan to commit to an action plan. This plan is a list of the things that you must do to achieve your goals. Now, every day, go over the list in your mind and look out for opportunities that will present themselves, for there are thousands of opportunities that we have not even dreamt about yet. Keep your mind and eyes open and keep searching, for these opportunities are everywhere. If you have found one, ask yourself, "How could I take this chance and seek more answers to my questions?" Keep asking questions and the answers will reveal themselves and before you know it you will find what you are looking for. And that is knowledge.

This is just a sample of what a "shopping list" for success will look like. This is not grouped according to duration. However, this will give you an idea of how to plan out your success story. Try it out and see what wonders this tiny list will bring about in your life.

So, how is your reading journey so far? Have you started drawing up your list of things to be achieved? These are just the first two steps and, as they say, that's two down and a lot more to go. If you read on, you will discover that there are more obstacles to conquer, and more things to consider in attaining success.

After envisioning the future and drawing up a list of things you want to achieve, you are ready to move on to the next step. Trust me; as you go along the list, you will realize that the road to success is never easy. As long as you have a way through which to achieve success, it is attainable. So, if you are ready to read on, I invite you to do so.

It is not wrong to believe in something. It is wrong; however, if all you have is your belief.

STEP 3

KNOWLEDGE IS POWER

Knowledge is power. I do not know about you, but personally I think this is a very appropriate title for this chapter. Why? Because knowledge is vital to achieving success. I know that such a statement is too general, even for my taste. So, allow me to explain.

I remember a scene from the animated movie *Hercules*. In the scene, Hercules was in a gorge, standing face to face with the Hydra. At first, Hercules started wrestling with the Hydra and, eventually, cut its heads off. But as he chopped off each head, three more heads grew out. In short, the Hydra grew so many heads that Hercules realized that he should stop cutting off the heads. So, instead of using his sword to slice off the Hydra's heads, he used his strength to break down a part of the mountainside, which eventually crushed the Hydra.

Now, I wish to use this example in explaining my point. You see, many of us simply hack away everything: money, opportunities, even the manner in which we face our Hydras. I realized at one point that I was battling my Hydras using the wrong tactics. The knowledge I am referring to is not just the vast amount of information stored in the brain. To me, knowledge is also being able to determine how best to defeat your Hydras without making them grow more heads.

Success is like battling it out with a Hydra. You have to know how to achieve victory and the only way to achieve victory is by knowing how best to conquer your monsters. The best way to achieve success is to know how and where to begin and how to execute the necessary actions for the attainment of your goals.

For me, the unending pursuit of knowledge is good. I believe that when people are determined to defeat their monsters, they do conquer them. So, learn new ways by which you can succeed because knowledge is power.

STEP 4

LET THE SHIP SET SAIL

Now that we have discussed the blueprint for success, I would like to talk about the factors that will equip you with the right weapons to strengthen your arsenal. When utilized in your pursuit for success, these will ensure that your achievement of success will be very enjoyable.

Some of these aspects of a person's life will prove to be commonplace. To many people, simply psyching up yourself to believe that you will succeed is not sufficient, people need that extra kick, if you get my drift. So, I would like to begin discussing these factors one by one. Again, I ask you to journey with me, as I take you from one aspect to another, one reality to another.

STEP 5

FAILURE LESSONS

There are moments when I feel that this cliché is too common, and that its common nature strips away any psychological and emotional reaction that people may have upon reading this statement. But in this case, I will have to make an exception. I seem to be left with no other choice than to use these frequently utilized words of wisdom, as I am unable to find other statements to justify my claims.

It is safe to say that everybody has committed at least a single mistake in their life, and that mistake is a downfall. People do not often realize this, but every time we feel disappointed about something, or feel regrets, those are downfalls as well. In life, there are often regrets and disappointments that we cannot seem to move on from. These unresolved issues cause us to become emotionally stagnated. In short, we have not gotten up from our falls.

This is one main reason why people do not succeed in life. Because of that emotional and probably psychological stagnation, people second guess themselves. Instead of determining the reasons or factors that have contributed to failure, most people prefer to wallow and stay in a slump, blaming the world or Lady Luck. Poor world and poor Lady Luck! It is quite strange that people should blame their misfortunes on inanimate objects or nonexistent beings.

In my opinion, failures are not supposed to be equated to deadweight or excess emotional baggage. For me, failures do not point to our inabilities, but indicate our potentials. Failure, in my perspective, is not the absence of success. It is, however, the means by which success is attained. If you fail, welcome the failure, for it teaches you what not to do next time. Sometimes, making a mistake is the best way to learn. It gives you an idea of how and what you are going to improve the next time around. In this sense, I turn my failures into "postponed successes" or, should I say, "Successes in the making."

When you walk, jog or run along the road to success, the time will come when all of us must fall or stumble. At times, we scrape our knees, and in some instances we are simply covered in dirt. Not to worry, for even if you fall, the road will still be there for you to run on. So get up, dust the dirt off and run towards your dreams once more.

Ok, you have tried many things in life and you have failed in many. That is fine.

Nature does not give up. The sun rises more than 93 million miles away from us, but every day without fail it does its job. The clouds protect the earth from the sun's rays, but the sun does not care if the rays are blocked by the clouds; it is constant without fail 365 days per year. Do you have what it takes?

Seeds travel with the wind for thousands of miles across this vast planet, but wherever the little seed lands, it begins the process of germination. Some die and others survive, but the process continues as plants continue to produce seeds year after year.

The laws of nature are relentless; there are no boundaries. It will continue to push ahead every single day with all forces necessary to keep the planet in momentum, so that life will continue, with it providing everything for sustenance.

The lesson here is that failure is a part of the process of becoming better. When you fail, you learn the cost of failure. Some will pay a higher price than others, but it teaches us how not to fail the next time around.

You see, I have had many, many failures in my life, made many foolish mistakes and indeed continue to do so today. I am far from being perfect, but I continue to learn every day, and I hope you will continue to do the same also.

You may now be wondering what comes next. I honestly have no clear analogies in my mind to describe the next stage. I am trying to find more appropriate scenarios, but I believe that this will best explain my thoughts: Achieving success is like an onscreen relationship between a man and a woman.

You might think that this is too analytical, but as I was thinking of what to write next, this was what came into my mind first. Let us try to consider what we have learned so far and liken it to relationships. First, we envisioned success, which may be equated to a guy having in mind an ideal girl, or vice versa. Next, we have to acquire knowledge to be able to determine how best to achieve success. This also happens when a guy tries to get to know the girl, hoping to find common things that they may talk about. Third, we have made a checklist for success. Some guys like to make checklists in terms of where to go on dates, and the like. Then we let the ship sail, which is what happens when a guy or a girl expresses his or her emotions to the other through simple gestures such as roses, chocolates, or fancy gifts. Failures enter the relationship when a guy or a girl is turned down, or if one's feeling of love or admiration is not reciprocated.

This is usually the time for popcorn, chocolates, beer nights and that much abused sentence: "It's time to move on."

Failure is a part of the method to achieve success.

STEP 6

MOVING ON

In every relationship, it is vital that one should try to move on when the relationship ceases to be productive, or if there is no possibility of being in a relationship. When one aspires to become successful, one should keep in mind that the road to success is filled with land mines known as failures. When one steps on a land mine, it will always explode. The question is: what do you do next?

In our pursuit of success, we may find ourselves struggling to achieve our goals. When we fail to achieve them, it is not wise for us to discontinue the journey. We have to move on. Moving on does not mean that we simply have to leave our bags and continue the journey. Moving on means that we have to bear with us the lessons we have learned from our errors, so that we are able to avoid making them a second time.

Moving on also means that if a particular dream is not working for you, then it is time for you to let go of it and start working on your next dream.

The world we live in does not pop out of a comic book. We live in a world where we are made out of flesh and bone, not ink and paper. In the fairytale world, we can wish upon stars and have fairy godmothers. In our world, we wish upon candlewicks and icing. In their world, the sky is the limit. In our world, everything has its limits. So, when you stumble because of your limitations get up and move on and do not forget to bring your bag of wisdom with you.

Let us begin with self confidence.

CHAPTER 2

SELF-CONFIDENCE

"Never bend your head. Always hold it high.
Look the world straight in the face."

~Helen Keller

Some say that confidence is the ability to smile even in the face of fear itself. Our fears are the bedtime monsters that haunt us in particular moments of our lives, and among those fears there is one fear that is quite common among people, the fear of self.

Can you remember the first time you delivered a speech in front of the whole class? Can you remember what it felt like to have them looking at you as though they were waiting for you to make a mistake? Do you remember your sweaty palms and trembling knees? I do. In most cases, when people are asked to deliver a speech, they want to head out the door, or ask for the speech to be given to somebody else.

We are afraid of ourselves. We are afraid to discover our strengths, to determine our weaknesses, and to embrace change. As a result, we are afraid to live fully. We are in constant struggle with ourselves, because we have aspirations that we wish to grab hold of. Because of our fear, we are unable to push ourselves to our limit or to even be near our limit which is ironic, given the fact that most of us are also afraid of failure and disappointments. So, the question is: How do we conquer this fear?

First, we must acknowledge the enemy, which in this case is the fear. We cannot fight or conquer an invisible enemy. Second, we must keep in mind that we are stronger than our fears and that no matter how ugly the beast of fear is, we are well equipped to conquer that beast. Finally, we must always fight the beast as best as we can and with all our might.

Daniel Maher once said, "Confidence is courage at ease." This courage is not the absence of fear. This courage is not shown through swordfights, or bucklers, or spears. No, this courage is something much more subtle. If we are to discuss courage, then it is in the quiet acknowledgement of fear. Being able to admit that we are afraid is courage in itself, because courage is the ability to do what is right, even in the presence of fear.

So how does self confidence enter the scenario? Okay, let's look at it this way: If you acknowledge that you are afraid, then you know how to fight it, and you will fight it. When you conquer your fears, then you can walk on with your head held high, look the world in the eyes and say: "I AM VICTORIOUS, FOR I AM CONFIDENT."

I think that questions that start with *what* are very specific, for they require a singular answer. These answers are definite, and there are no arguments. But it is not sufficient that we only know *what*; we also have to know *why*. I am no expert in terms of self confidence. So, I must refer to other sources of information. I find these very helpful and very comprehensive, and it is for this reason that I wish to share them with you.

What is fear? It is a feeling that is deep within; it affects every muscle in the body and do not forget that you could be paralyzed by the very notion of feeling fear. It could make you do nothing or make you do crazy things. So, will you let fear possess your life? Absolutely not. Do not let it keep you back.

Overcoming fear is like slaying the beast; once you overcome fear, you begin to win. So take advantage of this negative emotion and face it to overcome it. Let us recreate a new beginning, create new dreams, take some simple tips and move ahead.

Building your self confidence will always be a personal battle. The tips that people provide will only serve an external purpose. Ultimately it is up to you, whether or not you wish to improve your self confidence.

Now that we have started the discussion about self confidence, I wish to add that self confidence is not simply an internal exercise. Once you begin to feel that little sprout of confidence in you, do not stop there. Eventually, that sprout will grow, and you will feel confident inside. Since we are talking about success, it is also essential that we discuss exuding confidence.

Once you begin to develop your self confidence, you have to remember that it is not enough to *feel* confident. It is also important to *look* the part. The image you project must match the persona you wish to portray. It is the same reason you do not wear your pj's to work.

I wish to share a few tips regarding image building. These tips, coupled with the tips on self confidence, will ensure that you not only *feel* confident you will *look* confident as well. In addition to remembering to keep your shoulders and back straight, take a peek at these simple points:

CHAPTER 3

LOOKING THE PART

Here are the tips I wish to share with you so that you may build a good image:

1. Whatever clothes you may wear, formal or casual, make sure that they are neat and clean.

It is very important that people see that your clothes are neat and clean, so that they will not get the idea that you are sloppy and irresponsible. Clean and neat clothing will allow you to look professional and will give people the impression that you are somebody with whom they can discuss business.

2. Dress appropriately and remember age appropriateness is key.

For any occasion, it is important that you dress appropriately. I do not mean that you simply dress for the occasion. It is also important that you dress according to the people you will be with. I remember a scene in the movie *Erin Brockovich*, where Julia Roberts was reprimanded by her boss regarding her outfit, as everyone else in the office was looking at her. This is a typical example of why people should dress appropriately. People will not have a good impression of you if you wear tight miniskirts or ripped jeans and revealing clothes when you report to work. Such clothing is meant to be worn when you are out with your friends or perhaps not at all, but not when you are at work. So, make sure that you match your outfit with the occasion to avoid any untoward remarks.

3. Make sure that your make up or aftershave is subtle.

When looking at accomplished women in the field of business, one may see that they are not layered in makeup and perfume. There are women who are successful and wear lots of makeup, but I would presume that they are celebrities who need to wear makeup to serve their purposes. They need to wear lots of makeup because it is what is needed of them. Too much makeup is not really eye friendly, especially when you are working in an office. Given the lighting conditions and the working environment, it is best that you keep the application of makeup to the basics. This will provide a little tint and contrast, but just so it improves your facial characteristics. As a guy, I prefer to look at woman's natural beauty rather than the beauty that is riddled with too much cosmetic improvement. A woman's beauty always shows through her presentation and confidence. Same goes to men, go easy on the aftershave as too much is not smart.

4. Your hair should be well groomed.

They say that a woman's hair is her crowning glory. I would say it is the same for a man. With the exception of men who prefer to have their hair shaved off, it is vital that both men and women should keep their hair kempt. If what they say about a woman's hair is true, then we cannot afford to have unruly crowning glories don't you agree? If your hair is not neatly combed, then it will appear as though you just got out of bed and are not ready to work, or have rushed to work. This projects irresponsibility or laziness, which is not good for you if you want to be successful.

5. Take care of your footwear, and have shoes repaired if necessary.

Once you have made sure that your clothes are clean and neat, it is time to check the condition of your footwear. It is vital, if you want to project a successful image, that you present the entire package. It will not be much of a successful image if you have nice clothes but tattered footwear. So, make sure that your shoes are in good condition. Check for tears or defects when you purchase them. Men should make sure that they shine their shoes (if they are leather), and women need to make sure to clean their footwear whenever possible.

6. Do not over accessorize.

Some men and women prefer to be over accessorized. This is not a good look, as it appears juvenile. It is best that you keep things to the basic accessories such as a wristwatch, necklace and bracelet. Fewer accessories will do wonders for you.

Now that self confidence has been discussed, I believe that you already have an idea as to how to develop yours. It is in practice that the mastery of this particular aspect will be manifested. If you are afraid to talk in front of a crowd, try practicing in front of a mirror, or telling jokes to a group of friends, start small and then see where that takes you. You now have an idea how to feel and look confident. Conquer your fears by facing them.

I think it is time that we move on and discuss the other aspects. Once you have developed a sense of confidence, it then becomes vital to note that when talking about success, faith is another aspect. Many people would like to place their fate in the hands of their religious leaders, and therefore they put their success in the hands of other people. Success is a personal matter, and I would like to free people from certain paradigms.

So, let us move on to the next aspect, which is FAITH.

CHAPTER 4

FAITH

It is worth noting that faith is indeed a vital aspect of success. People have high regard for their faith. Karl Marx termed faith as "The opium of the people." Now, the question is: Why? In what way is it an opiate? I would like to explain, so please allow me to express my opinions regarding this matter.

Once upon a time, the church and the state were considered a unified entity. Although they served different purposes, they had a similar sense of hierarchy. During that period, the government was under fire due to instability. It was for this reason that people were inclined to lean on their faith as a means of alleviating the dire situation they were facing. As much as this is similar to the present time, there is one significant difference the state and the church are no longer unified. Whatever successes one attained, the other was in no position to meddle with its success because they no longer shared a connection.

It is in this context that I would like to project a particular scenario to best explain my stand in the matters of faith. There are moments when people approach their religious leaders and ask that they pray for their success. Being people of the faith, the religious leaders gladly agree. Let me ask you this question: What will their prayers do that your own faith will not provide you?

This is the flaw which I see in that scenario. We place the outcome of our endeavours on the intercession of somebody else. Most people simply call on their faith and do nothing afterwards and this is wrong. We think that God will provide everything for us; that we are no longer required to act and move. It may be a slap in the face, but things do not work that way. Your religious leaders are people just like you and they have no special pass or easier access to God than you do. If you will then seek your guidance from God and remember that you must work to achieve your success.

You have the power within you, which you may not be aware of. You are the master of your own fate, and if you want to have success delivered to you, then I suggest that you take action to make sure that happens. Even if a whole multitude of people were to kneel and pray for you, it would be of no use if you refuse to act upon your own fate. Life is governed by choices, and your fate is not a premeditated course of life. It is the product of the numerous choices which you have or will make in your life.

I will repeat this line: It is not wrong to believe in something. It is wrong; however, if all you have is your belief. Success does not come to those who sit around and wait. It comes to those who work hard. Do not get me wrong; I am not saying that having faith is, in itself, a form of complacency. I simply believe that, instead of spending most of your time going to temples or churches, you should work hard to achieve your dreams. I tell you, you will go a longer way.

CHAPTER 5

THE POWER OF THOUGHT

"You have powers you never dreamed of. You can do things you never thought you could do. There are no limitations in what you can do except the limitations of your own mind."

~Darwin P. Kingsley

A person's mind is one of the most powerful imaging systems in the world. There are endless possibilities inside the mind of a person, and if we harness that, then success is just a stone's throw away. In truth, I look at life as a state of mind. I believe that life's circumstances are merely products of our thoughts. People may argue that destiny is an existent reality. I wish to pose a question, then: If there is such a thing as destiny, then why are we given the chance to choose? I think that the term *destiny* is overrated.

In daily living, people are fond of using the phrase "That's life" or "Life wanted it that way." Isn't it strange that life can choose but you can't? Human beings have been granted the ability to rationalize and choose. If this is unspent, do we still qualify as human beings? I guess not. My friends, I mentioned a while back that you have the power to create your own destiny, and I will stress that once again. Do not leave everything to fate, because nothing happens out of thin air. Everything is fuelled by action and reaction, as Newton would have it. That's the first law of thermodynamics, and it may be applied to our day-to-day living. If somebody did something that offended you, then your initial reaction would be anger or annoyance. It is the same with success.

If we act towards success, then it will be attained. If you want to be somewhere in a few years, then you have to start with a single step, which will lead to more and more steps. We often hear the saying "Nothing is impossible." I agree with that. If you can conceptualize it in your mind, then you are able to do it. If you visualize yourself as a successful businessman in five years' time, then you will act upon it. You will tell yourself that you will be that in five years' time. This will be your motivation.

It is the same with olden-day wars, where swords and shields were used. It was usual for the military leaders to stand before their men and make morale boosting speeches. Because they set the thinking of their men into a fighting mode, their men become even more motivated to fight that war. Likewise, if you tell yourself that success will be attained, then you will see it realized.

Your thought is the engine that moves the body forward; it is the power plant that drives your passion forward; it is the energy generating station. If you think of searching for a job, but you have no education, your next thought is that it is best to get some more education to qualify for this job. If you do not do so, how else will you get the job legally? I do not mean through bribery, family contact and so on. It is pure in its very origin. Give it a try; it is simple. Create energy giving thoughts, and your life will be filled with more possibilities than ever. Not everything is going to work out for you, but you must continue on that path to obtain a positive mental attitude.

Be very focused and crystal clear, and the power to materialize your dreams will be far greater than ever. On your quest, you will meet people of different backgrounds, get to know where they started, the obstacles they went through in life, the life lessons they learned, and their advice to get you to the next level. Always ask for help when in need.

In pursuit of success, your best weapon is your mind. It possesses knowledge and vision, both of which are effective weapons. Once used, you will find that you have power beyond what you can imagine and that power is the power of thought.

We discussed earlier that one's perception of success is vital, but how do we come across this perception? Perception is not an inherent trait. Your perception depends on you. It is in that sense that I wish to discuss the power of thought.

They say that the average human only makes use of a small portion of their brain for normal daily functions, like computations. I am not here to tell you to tap into the bigger portion. I am here to help you see that if humans are able to carry out their daily functions by using only a small part of their conscious brain, then it is possible to psych yourself to become successful.

Give it a try. Allow yourself to perceive a successful future. Visualize yourself achieving the things you want to achieve. There is nothing wrong with that. Do this on a daily basis and you will find that you are slowly realizing your aspirations. You have got the power to create and destroy, because you have the power to think.

Now that we have discussed all of the details, we need to discuss what happens next. As they say, success is a persistent urge to improve what is insufficient and maintain what is enough. We have gone from thoughts to confidence to some other aspects of success. I believe that we have basically dealt with the lion's share of ideas and opinions.

Now, you may ask me, where do we go from here? As we already know a huge deal in terms of success, it is now time to put it into practice. All the steps, tips, and ideas I have presented will be justified given that this last topic will be maintained. Whatever method, tip, or idea you wish to go with, it is vital that this last thing be observed, as this is probably one of the most important things to keep in mind and put to use.

Ladies and gentlemen, I would like to introduce you to my friend CONSISTENCY.

CHAPTER 6

CONSISTENCY: THE MAGIC POTION

"There must be consistency in direction."
~ W. Edwards Deming

There must be consistency in direction and persistence towards a vision. I can find no other statement that best fits my justification. It is my honest opinion that it is this statement that holds ground when talking about consistency.

We all have dreams, and we all have our wishes. It is a known fact that this reality exists. We dream when we are asleep and we have dreams that occur to us even when we are awake. Indeed, we all have something that our hearts desire. However, numerous queries still stand: What do we do with that dream? Do we allow it to simply stay a dream or do we strive to achieve it? We all try to achieve those dreams. In the nooks and crannies of our conscious and subconscious mind, we all strive to get what we dream of. Sadly, not everybody gets the opportunity to hold those dreams in their hands. The question is: Why?

What did we do wrong? What did we leave undone? These are just common questions we ask ourselves. It's as if there is always something that we have not done, or it is always a question of what we did wrong. I believe that the tips I gave will take out the question of what you did wrong. One question remains unanswered: What did I leave undone? That is what I will address.

In our willingness to realize our dreams, we forget that it is not a matter of doing what you must *now*, but a matter of *always* doing what you must. We are amateurs who are fond of going on success marathons. What do I mean when I say "success marathons?" As a beginner, one would think that a marathon is simply about speed. So, when the go signal is on, we speed off like there is no tomorrow. We run as fast as we can, as we try to outrun everybody else. Then you are hit with muscle cramps. You feel tired, and it feels as though you are running out of air. Pretty soon, you have no other choice but to stop for a moment to catch your breath. That is what we do in order to become successful, and that is exactly what happens to us in the long run, we grow tired.

Many people around the world live mediocre lives. Why is this so? In fact, they say that most of the world's wealth is owned by about 10 per cent of the people. Have you ever wondered how this is possible? Research has shown that many people have worked extremely hard over several generations, some were born into wealthy families, and others have a talent through which they have become rich (but this is very few out of the 6 billion people living on our planet).

Sometimes, people do everything possible to achieve success but it never comes. Something you need to know is that in nature the rule is always broken. What I mean is, if you have the perfect situation for growth such as enough sunshine, moisture, nutrition, and good seeds, I bet you that there will be seeds that will not grow and develop into seedlings and a become a full grown plant or tree.

The lesson here is not to be discouraged when you have made the best effort and did not get the results you had been looking for. Always tweak and experiment if things are not working out your way. When I started a weight-loss program, at first I lost an amazing 20 lbs, but after the second month I stopped losing weight or lost very little. I decided to throw some more exercises into the program and then work a bit harder and longer, and I was sure that the plan would work, guaranteed. Now, how did I have so much certainty? I have read what a lot of other people did on blogs about weight loss, and I wanted to give it a try. The thing is that I still had a goal in my mind, and did more research to help me get there because I was determined.

The reason I am telling you this is because I want you to understand that I am an ordinary person who makes mistakes, and that some things do not always work. In my life, I have had many failures, and still do up to this day. I learn when I make mistakes and, sometimes, I repeat them; but it costs me time and money, so I realize that this mistake is costly. I am older now than before, and one may think that with age comes wisdom. It does, to a certain point, but we all screw up once in a while.

So, what do we do, then? The first thing to do is to stop thinking that success is a marathon. You are not competing with other people. In truth, you compete with no one but yourself. Second, you need to understand that, in running towards your dream, dashing for the finish could give you cramps and will hinder you in achieving your goal. I suggest that you start jogging first, and then gradually increase your speed to go faster. Once you have reached your desired speed, the key is to maintain it. Do not allow yourself to get cramps and get tired in the early part of your sprint. Do not try to get ahead immediately, because you are simply running against yourself. Only your personal prejudices, coupled with your fears, will hinder you in achieving your goal. So, break away from them and you can be assured that you will win against yourself in your personal race towards success.

CHAPTER 7

MEDIOCRITY

Another thing which is worth noting is that people prefer to become mediocre. We always settle with what is sufficient, and we do not try to set a high standard. We content ourselves with simply having what is acceptable, rather than exceeding the expectations. People complain about feeling small in the office, around friends and even around family, but it is worth noting that these people create the very net that holds them captive. They shackle themselves by their standards, and they end up feeling insignificant.

Mediocrity kills self confidence, because mediocrity will only give you mediocre results. I will give you an example. If a man sees himself only as a mailroom man, then that is all that he will strive for. He will only strive to be a mailroom man. Now, I am not saying that there is something wrong with being a mailroom man. What I am saying here is that humans are built for much better things, and that second guessing their abilities will only result in the wilting of one's self confidence. That is what we have to avoid.

Now, let's go back to the mailroom man. Imagine if the employee sets his standards a bit higher and, say, settles for an associate's position. That is higher up the organizational chart, but he is still able to achieve it. That is the magic behind setting your standards high. This will also apply to students. If a child simply aims to pass a course, then that child will only exert the effort required to achieve a pass. But let us consider the larger scheme of things. What if that child aimed higher? What if the kid set standards to become one of the top students in the class? Wouldn't he exert more effort to achieve that? I have faith in the ability of humans to rationalize and analyze. I believe that nobody is born insecure, they become insecure. That is what we need to fix.

So, let us compare the two scenarios. If a student who aims for a pass encounters a bit of a setback, then the student is prone to failing the subject. In some countries, the passing mark is 75 per cent. Now, if a student aims to reach just that, a setback might drag her grades to 74 per cent, which is already a failing mark. In this case, that 1 per cent cost a lot. If a student aims to reach 90 per cent and encounters a certain setback, which will again cost another 1 per cent, then it will bring the mark down to 89 per cent. Now, that is not bad at all, and it is still an above average mark. In this case, your 1 per cent did not cost you a lot, and at the end of the day you will still feel great having achieved 89 per cent. It is simply a matter of understanding that setbacks are bound to happen and how you handle them is up to you. Let me ask you this: Which would you rather have, 74 or 89 per cent?

This also applies to those who are already professionals. If you second guess your abilities, then what will you achieve in 10 years? Not much, I guess. If you change your standards, I believe that you will work harder and that, my friends, is what will bring you success. Understand that some things are bound to go wrong, and that your preparations will play an important role. Realize, as well, that, should you fall short of your high standards, better is one step short of best. Should you not achieve the best, at least you are left with something better than what is simply good. If you asked me, I would rather walk around with something better than with something which simply amounts to "good."

CHAPTER 8

BREAKING FREE

We have come to the concluding chapter on success. We have gone through quite a journey, and I see no other topic to end this aspect with, but this one. You have learned to break free from your internal bondage. This time, I will tell you how to break free from external captivity, known as the negative forces.

What are the negative forces, and how do they affect my journey towards success? Good question. Imagine driving along a winding road on a rainy day. Now, during those instances, one would consider the trip to be quite risky, given that the road is slippery and treacherous. Your innermost fears are your internal bondages, and in this scenario your external captivity would be the slippery and winding road. Because of your fear of those external constraints, you are forced to withdraw and put off driving towards your destination for another day. Do not get me wrong; I am not telling you to drive along winding roads on a rainy day all the time. This is merely an analogy. My thoughts rest on the fact that I acknowledge the dangers of driving in those conditions, and that it is not something I advocate. My purpose is simply to show you that the world's impression on you, coupled with all the comments, and criticism, and negative influences are huge road blocks which you have to break through; there are times when you need to get there because of a sense of urgency and you must act.

I understand that this is not a task for a child. This is a rather tedious task but once completed, you will feel the effects of being free from prejudices. Now, the question is: How do you break free from these chains? Let me share some tips with you.

First of all, you need to straighten out your priorities and have a clear perspective of how you are going to achieve it. This will give you the opportunity to do a self assessment and determine whether or not you truly know what is right and what is wrong. It will allow you to identify the things that are beneficial and useful in the achievement of your dreams and things that will endanger your chances of being successful.

Second, you need to stay away from the negativities which surround you. If you are surrounded by people who do not influence you in a good way, then stay away from them. If you feel that you are better off being solitary, then do so. It is better to be alone and free than to be in a shackled group.

Lastly, it is good to go back and review your progress, as well as your journey. It is human nature to make mistakes. That is something I acknowledge and that is also the reason why evaluations are important. Talk to yourself in a manner that is most comfortable to you. You may do it by meditating, talking to your reflection in the mirror, or through mental conversations. Look at your life from your point of view and see what needs improvement, what need to be taken out, and what should be added.

These are simple tips which people can follow easily. These are tips which we may hear from our friends. Most of the time, we ignore them. Trust me they work like a charm.

Success is not the only reality in the world. There are more out there, lots more. And if I was to discuss them all, I am afraid that it may take us forever. Lucky for us, we only have a few prominent realities, which we need to focus on. The next reality I wish to discuss is Change.

They say that change is the only constant thing in this world, and that everything is subject to change. I could not agree more. We all change, in one way or another. We grow older, thus changing our biological state from young and vigorous to aged and rather sluggish. We change from being toddlers with nothing else in mind but playtime and toys to professionals, with toys, who think about the stock market, taxes, and wages. You see everything in life changes at one point or another. It is unstoppable, and it is the only thing in this world that makes even the temporary duration of life exciting.

So, allow me to take you on another journey through change. Let us discover what changes we have gone through, and what changes we will go through in the future.

PART 2

THE LIFE LESSONS

"Your work is to discover your world,
and then with all your heart give yourself to it"

~Buddha

Life lessons are everywhere. We go from day to day, moment to moment, and at the end of it all we ask ourselves: What happened?

Life could be beautiful to enjoy; it is always about the opportunities that we take at the right moment. If the desire is strong, then change will come to your life; if not, you will fall on the wayside and will have to play the catch up game, and time will have passed by. I will stress that one of the reasons for writing this book is to at least give one person a chance to make it.

You can make a difference in people's lives in some ways. Be a friend, help someone in need, be generous in your praises, build people up and do not tear them down, do something that will make your heart remember these small moments. Life, if planned properly, will take you to that destination even faster so do something for yourself; love yourself, and you are on your way.

Life lessons are like road signs. The people who take the time to notice these signs are able to drive safely. They are aware of what's to come, because they have received prior warning. This is quite the same in terms of living. Our life lessons act as signs on our roads. They serve as our guide, especially when we are on unknown territory. We know what to watch out for, thus eliminating fear and intensifying our confidence to proceed through life.

CHAPTER 1

ACTIONS SPEAK LOUDER THAN WORDS

As far back as I can remember, people have always told me that it is important to accompany our dreams, aspirations, determination, and words with action. When I was a kid, people would always tell me that if I leave my dreams to remain as such, then they will never come true. Even as a kid, I felt that they had a point.

Looking back, I can definitely say that, though it might seem too cliché to mention, actions *do* speak louder than words. It is most certainly true. People have to realize that if one does not strive to attain his or her goals, then nothing will happen. Dreams remain dreams until action is introduced. In science, it is said that a ball in motion will continue to be in a constant speed of motion unless an external force is introduced.

This is an analogy that best justifies my point. Imagine that your dream is the speed of the ball. It will go unchanged unless an external force is introduced. So, if an external force is not introduced to your dreams in order to start a change, then your dreams will remain constant; in that sense, your dreams will remain the same.

So, consider this: Allow yourself to move and act upon your dreams. If you want to realize the dreams you hold dear, then I suggest that you do something to make sure that happens. And remember, actions speak louder than words.

PART 3

CHANGE

Our lives are governed by forces, and we are compelled to subject ourselves to these forces. Gravity prevents us from floating away and so do the other scientific phenomena. We are surrounded by things that stay the same despite the location, the circumstance, and even the beholder. We wake up every day knowing that when we get out of the bed, our feet will always touch the ground. Because of this, gravity is no longer an issue, nor is it something new. Because gravity is consistent wherever we go, I think it is safe to say that it becomes uninteresting. This extends to other things, such as heat, electricity, friction, and acceleration. Despite their rather intricate designs, they exist simply to be recognized as warmth, light bulbs, brake pads, and gas pedals. The intricacies no longer matter, because there is always a mundane exemplification of the aforementioned, and they are consistent in nature.

Let us talk about change. Every day, we come across consistent changes in our surroundings. The sun rises and sets, the wind blows from different directions, the waves crash and ebb, the tide rises and falls, people go from young to old, and so on. These are natural events, and we are witnesses to these processes. And although they may be as common as knowing that anything thrown into the air will eventually come down, we do know that the sun may not shine as bright tomorrow, and that the moon does not always show its face. Life is somewhat like the sun, or age, or waves, or tide. Life has its many changes, too, and it should not strike us as odd.

People often ask this question: Why do things have to change? Change is what makes life colourful. Change is what adds a bit of flavour to our existence, because it is through change that we are able to perceive a reality which is not premeditated. We, as human beings, follow a certain moral code but not a set of specific instructions. Change allows us to not eat in the same restaurant every day, or to wear the same clothes to work daily, or to follow the same routine over and over and over again. Change is what makes us argue over what shampoo to buy or what type of food to eat for dinner.

Yes, all of these things are a bit chaotic, but let us face it; these things are the spice of life. A life without change is like having a burger without patties or a salad without dressing. Everything just seems so plain and uninteresting. Now, some may argue that change is not always good. I agree. Not everything of everything is good. There are always two sides to a story.

It is important that we are wary of these changes, picking out only the points we will benefit from. One should not simply stick to established practices but seek out the new and improved ways of performing certain tasks. In the past, electronic typewriters did the job well; today people prefer to have their reports printed out. If boy-girl relationships were the only types in the past; thankfully people are more open minded now.

I would like to discuss these changes over the next few pages. So, come with me and let us dissect the world of change.

"Life can either be accepted or changed. If it is not accepted,
it must be changed. If it cannot be changed,
then it must be accepted."

~Anonymous

There are moments in life when we question the very nature of change. We have inculcated into our subconscious that if change works in our favour, then it is good, and if it does not, then it is bad. It has been our nature that every time Lady Luck smiles at us, we consider it a blessing, and when things change and turn out for the worst, then we consider this as a punishment. Have we tried to look upon our misfortunes as blessings as well? Some people are intolerant to change because it does not suit them, or they simply do not see themselves going in that direction.

This is a perfect image of a typical human life. We wish to flow in a particular direction, and then we complain if we have a tendency to veer away from our desired path. And I say that this is not correct. Why? There are external factors that we need to consider, and these external factors will somehow affect the ways in which we wish to conduct ourselves.

We possess a power that we do not know of. We have made men fly, we have made men travel faster, and we have harnessed the power of nature and channelled it to our gain. We have done all these and other things through the persistent desire to discover something new. In the course of a million or so years, men have gone from carving stone tools to making tools that make tools. I believe that whatever struggles we have now; we will conquer like we have conquered all the others. In order for us to hold in our hands the beauty of a consistently changing life, we have to free ourselves of our prejudices and doubts, for we are human beings capable of great things.

Let me give you an example. One person is in dire poverty and he wishes to buy a sports car. He is on a particular path and, because his poverty veers him away from his path, he complains and blames everybody else for his poverty. This example is not given so that I will impart a lesson that he must accept his poverty. No, it is not that. What I wish to impart is that for him to achieve his dream, he has to embrace change. In my opinion, poverty is not a state of financial difficulty. In my opinion, poverty is a state of psychological tolerance for mediocrity. A person will only be considered poor if he accepts that state and wishes to do nothing to alleviate himself from the situation and the environment.

In this sense, for that poor man to own a sports car, he has to embrace change, change in his mindset, in his living conditions, in his determination, as well as in all other aspects relevant to the achievement of his dream. If he wants to own that car, he has to introduce something more than what he has. This is not an example of going beyond one's limits. I am showing you that if a person wants to succeed, then he or she must acknowledge the fact that little adjustments or changes have to be made even on a daily basis, in order to make sure that when things become quite demanding, you are certain that you are able to adjust.

Nothing is impossible. You have the power to achieve the things that you have conceived in your mind. All it takes to reach them is a dream, fuelled by your determination to accept the changes and be better.

In ancient times, people carved symbols on stone and wrote on animal skin. Then paper was discovered, and people developed writing materials, and then followed the innovations that paved the way to our modern writing materials. Correspondence in those days was sent via footmen or couriers. Now, you may ask me: What is the significance of this review of the history of correspondence? This is to show you that changes do occur.

Nowadays, documents or files which need to be forwarded to another location are just a click away. Even if the recipient of your document or file is halfway around the world, you are certain that they will be able to receive the document just seconds after you send it. Convenience, speed and ease are very essential in today's world. The ability to comply within a short period of time is essential, and if one embraces that change then things will be a lot easier.

Though this may be a very timely change, I am not suggesting that you go out and embrace every form of change you can find. As I said, it is still important to choose which changes are beneficial to you. In your quest for self improvement and success, work with the changes that will help you achieve your dreams. I believe that adequate knowledge and proficiency in operating and manipulating modern day gadgets and equipment will aid you, as today's world is growing more and more technologically advanced.

As I write this book, I do not do it the old-fashioned way. I simply type away on my laptop, which I believe is easier and more convenient than writing my thoughts down by hand. As much as I respect written materials, it is also a fact that people prefer to use online or computer based materials. It seems as though people would rather pour over eBooks and blogs than pick up a paper printed book to read.

At this very moment, I begin to realize that soon enough people are going to download this book. If I took the time to laboriously jot down my thoughts, look for publishers, and secure copyrighting, it would be a long time before I got to see my work read by many people. So, I prefer to just push buttons on my laptop, have my thoughts translated into megabyte after megabyte of information, and still have my work read by many people. For me, time is of the essence, and since the situation warrants this being done as soon as possible, then I choose the method which will ensure just that.

CHAPTER 1

CHANGE AND CONSISTENCY

I do not wish to create a conflict between my previous talk about change and consistency. Trust me, both are essential. The consistency of our determination and goals, coupled with our constant persistence for self discovery through reinvention, will guarantee us a dream come true. I want you to understand that both exist not for us to choose which to favour. They are there so that we can realize that, though they may be a contradiction to each other, they are best when side by side.

I have laid my confidence into believing that, in order for people to achieve a particular type of consistency in their lives, a number of flexible, changing matters have to be dealt with first. What do I mean by this? Let's take cooking, for example. Before a person achieves the taste which his or her friends like, that delicious taste has gone through a tedious process of having the dish too salty, too sweet, too sour, too lumpy, too bland, and too spicy and so on. Before one decides to stick to a particular recipe, a series of trials and errors have been made.

Let us look at it in the perspective of change and consistency. Before we stick to a particular program, we have to keep in mind that life is a matter of trial and error, because its very nature is, in itself, relative. One cannot perceive the very nature of life to be absolute. We can have consistency in terms of work related activities, our favourite brand of t-shirts, or for any other aspect. However, one cannot have that with life, because the only consistent thing in life is change itself. Our trials and errors have no lifetime guarantees.

There have been numerous arguments regarding the very consideration of change. We have considered change as an opposition to consistency, and it may be considered, therefore, an inconsistency. We also hold that change is the only consistent occurrence. One cannot fully say that one object remains the same as time passes. So, what is change and consistency?

I thought about the very same thing and it dawned on me that, after centuries of human existence, after decades of research, scientific experimentation, and empirical claims, we have not explained the simple things. Oh, sure, we have explained why atoms split, why dinosaurs died out and why the world exists the way it does. Yet we cannot even determine the relationship between two very common and simple realities.

I bet that you have your own thoughts about change and consistency. It is because of this that I thought about my own definitions of change and consistency. If consistency is maintaining a particular routine, and change is the alteration of routines, then why is change considered a consistent entity? Is it not ironic that we should use one to modify the other? I say it is not.

As I mentioned on the previous page, I believe that they are best when side by side. They are, in my opinion, a cause and effect. It does not matter which is which. One can be sure that when one is the cause, the other is the effect. If a person's life seems to be too much of a routine, he or she is bound to look for a new experience. And when one person has gone through numerous job changes, or perhaps numerous relationships, then he or she is bound to want to stick with just one job or one relationship. There is no contradiction with these two realities. We are authors of that contradiction, although that contradiction is more of a personal issue than one created by these realities.

We create our own inner arguments and contradictions. It is our impulse that if we find something is not in tune with our wishes, we are bound to contradict. My thoughts have led me to question myself, "When have I considered reconciling my thoughts, ideas, and feelings with others?"

Try doing the same, and I assure you, you will realize a lot.

Having discussed how change and consistency can leave quite an impression on our lives, let us now begin to discover how we embrace these realities, for it is useless to stand by a belief in something existent.

It is a known fact that people are subject to change, as is everything else. We go with the flow and feel happy that we are "in." As we journey towards our dreams, we tend to stop by the roadside simply because we are confused by the signs of the times.

This confusion is what moves us away from our goal. As we go with the flow, we become no more than driftwood in a raging current. I am sure everybody has had an experience that is in some way related to going with the flow I know I did. It is because of this that I now impart to you my little seeds of wisdom, which I have gathered from my own experiences.

First, the nature of change is not bad. Change is a good thing because it helps us reinvent ourselves. Reinvention is also good because we become pliant, so to speak. That reinvention is also the means by which we discover a lot about ourselves. It is change that keeps us going; it fuels us to strive to become better people.

Second, change is constant. I know that we hear this all the time, but change is definitely a mainstay of life. Change is like an unseen force, which is also unstoppable, inevitable, and timely. Why do I say timely? I have come to realize that the decision to change always comes when people are at a certain crossroads in their life. It never comes before or after the crossroads; it is always there to meet and greet you as you decide where to go.

Lastly, change is important. It is important because when a person feels stagnated and bored, there is absolutely no spark of brilliance or interest in his or her mind. It is simply a feeling of being fed up about and burnt out by a routine which one finds dull and not stimulating in any way. When that happens, success slips from your fingers.

As I am done expounding my thoughts about change and consistency, I believe that it is now time to talk about how people can embrace these two factors into their lives. Our knowledge about change and consistency alone will not be of much help if we do not put it into practice. So, over the next few pages, I shall discuss how one can embrace change, and how one can use it to his or her advantage. I hope that you will find it helpful in your personal quest for a renewed you.

Let us now proceed to the next chapter.

CHAPTER 2

GIVE CHANGE
A GREAT BIG HUG

I trust that by now you already have an idea of why change is important. I prefer not to keep on reviewing the previous chapters, because my aim is for us to keep moving forward, not constantly go back. So, I will now give you my thoughts about how to embrace the changes in our lives, and how one can use this to his or her advantage.

There is a diagram made by a psychotherapist named Virginia Satir. It illustrates the levels of acceptance and their effects on the person as a whole. The diagram is a simple square divided into four parts: Status Quo, Resistance and Chaos, Integration and Practice, and New Status Quo.

I would like to explain the diagram according to my understanding, and I do hope that you will see its relevance to your own life. According to the diagram, a society—or in this case a person—starts out with a *status quo*. These are the things with which we are familiar. These are the things that we have accustomed ourselves to. This is also called the grey zone. Beside the grey zone is the red zone. This zone is called *resistance and chaos*, and between the red zone and the grey zone is a thin line called the *foreign element*. This foreign element is a trigger or a change agent which introduces something new to society, which leads to resistance and chaos. The resistance leads to chaos as people are unwilling to embrace the change which is being introduced to them. People are afraid to venture out of their safe zones because of the unknown, and that is quite a normal response except for the adventurous.

In my opinion, it is for this very reason that we refuse to embrace the changes in our lives. We are afraid that we may become incompetent, and therefore we choose not to favour the revisions, but rather to stick with the things we do best. If this is so, then our lives will be no better than a life lived with mediocrity as its creed. I think this is also one of the perks of change. Most of the time, changes are implemented for improvement not only in business, but also for oneself. A company that chooses to modernize its facilities aims to speed up the company's processes and, in turn, improve the employees' outputs. Workers who rely solely on their knowledge and intuition would find it quite a task to perform at the same level as workers armed with well equipped posts.

My point is that changes like these should be taken as constructive, not destructive, in nature. If one finds difficulty in adapting to a particular system of operation or to a particular activity, then it simply means that one's knowledge is insufficient. Changes are put to effect so that employees gather additional and current information and input, which they can use both in the professional and personal aspects. If one struggles to adjust to a newly implemented scheme, then it simply means that there is more to learn. If a person acquires more knowledge, then it makes them better at what they do. Now, that does not seem so bad, does it?

That brings us to field number three, *integration and practice*. As soon as one gets the gist of the ins and outs of a particular system, and if one has gathered enough knowledge to use in the workplace, then it is time for integration. The input you receive will not stay a mere input. Integration and practice have to be applied in your daily work related output, so that you can see the improvement in your work. Let me give you an example.

In ancient times, people made use of traditional medieval tools for farming. Not only was it a burden to the bulls at that time, it was also very difficult fro the farmer. They produced a lot of grain, but only enough to support the population of that time. Now, imagine if we had no tractors or irrigation methods. Let us imagine bulls trudging along farmlands, and let us imagine, if we must, a world where we have to consume only the exact amount of grain they produced at the time. I imagine that almost everybody would be hungry. Thanks to modernization, we now have tractors, irrigation systems, and numerous methods by which farming has been improved.

I am not here to say that the ancient method is ineffective. I am here to state that as time goes by, the demand for certain commodities and products eventually increases. In that sense, if we refuse to embrace certain changes, which will enhance production and all other economic processes, then a lot more people will go hungry, and convenience will be nothing more than a thing of the past.

Do you now see the significance of change? We may not always see the beauty of change. Let us keep in mind that our world is not moving backwards. It is in a constant search for improvements and innovations which will make work easier and will turn good results into better ones. Some things are not as bad as they seem.

After integrating the revisions into our daily lives, they will eventually develop into a routine. Once it becomes a routine, people begin to integrate that particular routine in their lives as well, and in so doing, you have created a brand new status quo. As the new status quo is instituted, the process will continue. New changes will be introduced; at first, people will refuse to accept them; then they will begin to integrate them in their daily lives and another status quo will be achieved. In this sense, we have now achieved consistency through change.

CHAPTER 3

INITIATING CHANGE

"Be the change you want to see in the world."

-Mahatma Gandhi

As much as people hate change, it is ironic to see them look for change. Recently, the world has borne witness to numerous protests against leaders who have been in office for far too long. People have gone to the streets in a rather bloody manner to urge their president to step down. It may appear strange that, after having been under a particular rule for quite some time, they ask for the leaders' resignation just now. Why have they not spoken up for all these years?

It may be remembered that in the Philippines, the people also went out on the streets to ask for the resignation of two of their Presidents. Both of these Presidents resigned. That particular moment gave others an idea that when a President or a leader is no longer able to perform their duties, then the people who put them in office may ask them to give up their post. In most countries, that is called sovereignty. In the Philippines, it was called the EDSA Revolution.

The very famous EDSA Revolution sprouted a seed of sovereignty in other countries. As you can see now, many Middle Eastern countries have followed the example set by the EDSA Revolution but only to a certain extent. Their call for their leaders' resignation has resulted in a bloody encounter with the military and the leaders non questioning supporters. In a sense, there is still a small seed planted by the example set by the Philippines.

We should do the same. If we wish to see change in our lives, in our schools, in our workplaces, then we should be an example to others. We should be the change that we want to see in ourselves, in other people and, hopefully, in the world.

Why do I encourage you to initiate change? Why do I ask you to start a movement in your life? I am a firm believer in the saying: "The journey of a thousand miles begins with a single step." I believe that in order for you to be able to get to that somewhere that you wish to be, you have to take that single step. To travel life as it is may already prove to be very difficult. But it is because of that tedious journey that one is able to experience the beauty of living, a living made even more beautiful by the little changes we introduce.

Talking about little changes and little steps, how do we determine which little steps to take? This is when good company and good tips come in. Change is usually introduced when there is a need for us to alter a routine which is not functioning as well as it used to. If we are to alter something, let us make sure that it is in our best interests. It is best that we carefully choose people whom we can ask for advice and tips, and make sure that, before we decide to introduce a change, we think it over many times.

I am no change guru, but I have little tips which have done wonders for me, and I hope that they will do wonders for you, too.

- Have a good set of values as your guide for change.

When we were little, people would always remind us what is right and what is wrong. Over the years, those reminders have learned how to communicate with us; they have become that little voice we know now as our conscience. This conscience is our front liner; it is the first one to remind us what is good or bad. Our decision to change may very well be influenced by that tiny voice, and I suggest that you listen to it.

- Your colleagues, friends and family are good sources of advice.

After consulting yourself, it is also important that you consult the people who know you well. Why is this important? The change you need to initiate may well be seen by everybody else but you. So, simply consulting yourself may not prove to be of much help, although this does not apply to every circumstance. Consulting your colleagues, friends and family will also allow them to evaluate whether the change you wish to implement is for the common good or simply for self improvement.

Although both present good intentions, it is still best to determine whether or not the people who are closest to you also find it pleasant and necessary. In the end, if you do wish to change, consulting them about it will give them a heads up about the things you wish to do.

- Keep in mind that you are the master of your life and the author of your fate.

You are the first one who can evaluate whether you need the change or not. You cannot please everybody, and in that sense, the only person you need to satisfy is yourself. This does not mean that you are to shut yourself off from the world. I am merely stating that you must have the final say on things. If you feel that the change you are proposing will lead to your overall improvement without jeopardizing relationships or stepping on people, then go ahead. You must be the one to initiate the change not other people.

- Tell me about your friends, and I will tell you how to change them.

In cases where you wish to change not yourself but the people around you, you must allow yourself to influence them, not the other way around. You must be steadfast in your convictions and beliefs, for they are without measure and of boundless value. If the small voice in your head tells you that it is time to do something about something, then do it. Be the change you want to see in the world.

These are simple tips on how one can begin initiating change. It always starts with you and with determination to amend and renovate in some way. These may not be the executive, black and white types of tips, but I assure you that they work. Each time I decide to alter something in my life, I make sure that I refer to these mental notes I call "tips." They have been very helpful to me, and it is for this reason that I share them with you. They are easy to do, and the nature of these tips is not very complicated. Let the alterations begin!

CHAPTER 4

LET THE WORLD KNOW

Once you have made up your mind that a change is needed, it is time to let the world know about it. At this time, consistency will be your best friend. For me to explain it better, let me give you an example.

In the movie *The Matrix*, Mr. Anderson (Keanu Reeves) was reprimanded by his superior regarding his tardiness. I believe this is applicable not only to Mr. Anderson but to many of us. We have been late for something many times. In most cases, this has cost us a lot. Now, let us jump forward a few frames to what I believe is a relevant scene to Mr. Anderson's ordeal in his workplace. Mr. Anderson wishes to get out of the car as it stops at an intersection. As Mr. Anderson opens the door, Morpheus (Laurence Fishburne) tells him that Mr. Anderson knows where that road leads to, and that it is not where he wishes to be. Now, for most of us, our interpretation may have been that he was just trying to get Mr. Anderson into the Matrix. I believe that there is a deeper implication than that.

I believe that Morpheus was trying to remind him that if he chooses to stay on the path he is currently on, nothing will change in his life. If he wishes to continue living a very mediocre and irresponsible life, then he will not be much of a benefit to himself. If he chooses to change, then he will become somebody.

That is very much what we all need to remember. If we consistently choose to take the same path of mediocrity, then it is time to make a u-turn. If we imagine Mr. Anderson symbolizing us in everyday life, then there is much to be learned. He chose the red pill and it changed his life. He became somebody in the world of Matrix. He was a program of immense strength, and people knew him and respected him. We can be like that. We can be of immense strength, and people will look up to us. The question is: How do we let the world know?

"The world" does not necessarily mean the great vastness of soil, water, and trees. I believe that the world is the environment you exist in. The world may include your workplace, your peers, your family, and your community. They are your world, and it is to them that you wish to show your change. If you are always late for work, then show your co-workers that you are a changed person by showing up for work on time or earlier. If you consistently get bad grades, then show that world you have changed by studying hard. These changes are non-consuming monetarily, and they will contribute to your well being. How? If you are commended for a good performance at work or school, it is natural to feel good about yourself. We require affirmation at least once a day. And since our human psychology requires that, we will maintain our good performance. It is like taking that red pill. It's a 'no turning back' pill, but one that is life changing.

The change you make will eventually show itself, and although those around you may find it new or strange, at least it is a good type of new and a good type of strange. It is a change which encourages responsibility and promotes the alleviation of one's self worth.

CHAPTER 5

MAKE IT A HABIT

They say that with time your routines become a habit. Now that we have stressed the importance of introducing good change in one's life, it is time to make the good changes a habit. As you begin to strive to constantly act according to the changes you have introduced, you will notice that it starts to become more of a routine. You report to work on time, consistently get good grades in school, and see other improvements. Once these have become a routine, they will eventually become your habit. Having these positive practices as one's habits is a good thing.

It is then your responsibility to make sure that it becomes a habit. It may seem difficult at first, but the long term effects are very beneficial.

They say that the most successful people are not those who claim to be knowledgeable about a particular task, but those who actually show up to accomplish the tasks. I agree. If you want to be successful at making a habit out of these good traits, then you must be there to do it.

One must realize that there are a lot of things in life that need remediation and alteration. It might be your outlook on love, on work, on school, on socializing, on family, and on other things you may find relevant. Because we are imperfect beings, we carry imperfections with us. It is our task to make sure that we endeavour to keep those flaws to a minimum and, therefore, change the ones we deem necessary.

Let us make our improvements a habit. Let us master the ability to make our lives, as well as the lives of other people, more pleasant and more fulfilled through the changes we make, coupled with the consistency we maintain.

Our journey through change is about to come to a stop. We have traversed a rather complex world of change, and I believe that we have absorbed as much information and as many tips as we possibly could.

The tips and statements I have made in the chapters I have written are my personal beliefs, which have provided very good results.

Friends, I hope that my chunks of wisdom have encouraged you to seek your own tidbits of learning. I hope that, as you read through the pages of these chapters, you were able to incur a sense of value for both the little and huge changes in your life. Always know that they are never antagonistic by nature; they depend solely on our ability to decide what is beneficial and good, and what is not.

Let us also keep in mind that our choices will always have an impact on our lives, and that if we wish to see ourselves turn from a scrawny caterpillar into a beautiful butterfly, then we have to make good choices, especially in the manner and the purpose in which we are to change.

Change in itself is never meant to remove or replace anything that is of value to us. It is simply there so that we may open our consciousness to possibilities and opportunities. The changes we encounter in our lives exist for the sole purpose of metamorphosis, and not demolition. Change is there to enhance and to beautify, and not to seek the destruction of our well being and our relationships. My friends, change for the better!

Now that we are done with Parts 2 and 3, I believe that it is time to take a breather and review what we have learned so far. We have gone from success, to life lessons, to change. You may ask me how they are related to one another.

At first view, they may seem irrelevant to each other. Upon close inspection and scrutiny, you will find that they are interconnected. You may find that I presented this deductively. I gave you an idea of what success is, and, starting at Part 2, I have been working my way along the path. I am breaking down success into its significant parts. Success is always a result, and not a cause. It is a result of life lessons put to good use, accompanied by constant revisions in order to attain the desired rhythm. The next parts of *The Roadmap to an Enriched Life* will showcase the many other facets of success. I am not here to divulge them just yet. For now, we are taking the time to see how branched out success can be, and that the attainment of success means the mastery of a number of other aspects.

So, let us think. Let us think of our experiences, which have led us to our current situations; you reading this book. Our experiences may include success, poverty, it may be psychological and emotional uneasiness; it may simply be doubts. While some may say that they feel okay and that nothing is wrong with them, the very denial of things going wrong is something that is wrong. As you read this book, I want you to think of those unfortunate circumstances, and I want you to visualize them going away. Bit by bit, I will do my best to let you see that the monsters you face are of your own making, and that you can make them go away at your will.

Friends, I invite you to read on . . .

So the big question now is: What's next? We have discussed success, life lessons and change in just a matter of almost 100 pages. There are now another 100 pages, more or less, within which you will find further aspects of success. These are the three most talked about aspects of success, and I feel that it is right to allot the lion's share of the book to these topics.

So, where do we begin? We begin with love. And no, not just boy-girl love, puppy love, or marital love. I will be discussing love from a different perspective, but with reference to those I just mentioned. We shall be discussing love bit by bit, and we shall delve into the very fundamentals of love and how it can be utilized for success.

Many of you may find it quite strange that love should be a recipe for success. Many of you would be surprised to know that love plays a huge role in success, because love is one of the prime movers of men and women alike. Of all the most commonly felt emotions, I believe that love is a favourite topic of discussion. Since this is a case, let us begin to talk about love.

PART 4

LOVE

INTRODUCTION

LOVE:
BY EVERY DEFINITION

Love has always been a universal topic. People create their own love quotes, love clichés, and love mottos. We love according to a certain code, a certain blueprint, if we must. Most of us learn to love in hopes of having that love returned by another person. Some of us love because of the mere satisfaction of it and some love out of obligation. Whatever our definitions or clichés or codes are, it all boils down to allowing ourselves to feel that emotion.

So, since people seem to be always in the mood when talking about love and all its technicalities, let us examine how civilization defines love. We shall discuss these clichés and how they may be applied in day-to-day living.

For some, love is an expression of generosity to others. Some may consider it to be respect, and others still consider it to be many other things. I believe that it is all that combined. It is merely a matter of who receives that love. It is in that sense that I wish to discuss the hierarchy of love. I wish to expound my thoughts regarding love.

In the next few pages, I shall be providing you with my mental notes regarding love. These are thoughts that have dawned on me while driving my car, taking coffee breaks, and even brushing my teeth. I believe that these thoughts have dawned on you as well, but you may be unaware of it. So, let us proceed to our discussion about love.

CHAPTER 1

LOVE:
STEP BY STEP

First of all, I believe that love is more than what we perceive it to be. We perceive love to be an emotion. I think that there is more to love than just the emotion itself. I believe that love is a process. It requires us to become familiar, if not very familiar, with the details. It is a process because, like all procedures, we cannot move on to other things without accomplishing what we need to in the moment.

So, if love is a process, then what are we supposed to do? We need to know where we begin. We have to start at square one. This square may be the basic square of love, but this is the most important step. It is what determines our ability to love the people in our lives. And before I do just that, I would like to share with you a line from a song: "Learning to love yourself, it is the greatest love of all."

I do not know if it is indeed the greatest love of all, for I know that many would disagree. So, I wish to simply consider it as a great kind of love. Why do I say this? That is what I will share with you in the next chapter.

CHAPTER 2

LOVING ME 101

"Love towards yourself is a romance that lasts a lifetime."
~Oscar Wilde

For as far back as I can recall, the people closest to me have always reminded me of one thing, love for oneself is highly important. At first, I never really understood why it was so significant. All the while, I thought that loving oneself first was nothing more than selfish. I preferred to give my love to other people rather than allot it for myself.

As time passed, I began to realize why it was significant: I cannot give love when I have no love in me to give. I guess that is pretty much why you have to love yourself first. They say that relationships fail because we tend to give more than we actually have.

So in this sense, I would like to ask you a question: "Do you love yourself?" This is not narcissism, this is simply the acknowledgement that *you* matter as well. I know that our morals, set by other people, tell us to always consider the common good and that selflessness is a good thing. I am not here to argue with that. I am here because I believe that, before you can give love, you have to have love inside of you.

We all look for ways to become selfless. Parents are living testimonies to that. They basically do anything humanly possible just to provide a better life for their children. I guess I am qualified to talk about that, because I am a parent as well. I would go through hell in order to make sure that my girls get the best out of life. My girls are quite grown up now, and are pretty independent. I know that they might not have as much need for my help anymore, now that they are living their own lives. They know that I will always be here for them.

All these things would not have been possible if I did not have a sense of self. Had I lost my love for self and value for life, I believe that you would not be reading this. Given that circumstance, everything would have been totally different.

So you see, what seems insignificant at first may prove to be very vital in the long run. We try to give as much of ourselves as possible to others, but we keep nothing for ourselves. We make it a point to orchestrate the best wedding proposal, the best engagement party or the best dinner date for two. But we never take the time to ask ourselves if we ourselves feel loved.

Here is my suggestion: Be in your most comfortable clothes. You may be sat in front of the television, you may be at the beach getting a tan, or simply in bed reading a good book. Do what you love doing and allow yourself to experience that every now and then. Go on a date with yourself and make sure that it is a date to remember.

People nowadays seem to have a lot to say when it comes to love. They appear to be experts on love, indeed, we all do. Isn't it quite strange that, despite our knowledge about love, we still find it hard to love the very person from whom love is supposed to emanate? The question to be asked at this moment is: How? How do we love ourselves?

I may not know a great deal about love. Perhaps I never will. I can borrow a few thoughts from others, knowing that two heads are better than one, and three heads are certainly better than two.

Before I began writing this chapter, I made it a point to dive into books and journals about love. I realized that if I were to talk about love, I should do so by appealing to the general sense of it all, given that our experiences of love are relative. So, in my research, and in my personal experiences as well, I have come up with a few tips on how we can love ourselves.

Tip #1: Learn to love yourself

When we fall in love with other people, it seems as though they become the most ideal person in the world. Their good traits are magnified, while their not so pleasing traits are lost in the whole magnifying experience. We do this almost on a daily basis with other people. How often do we do that with ourselves? We have to learn to look at ourselves in the mirror and tell ourselves those three simple words.

Now, I guess this step is difficult to accomplish. Why? It's because we find it difficult to do the second step. This is the reason why we have to search for the things that we love about ourselves so that it will be easier for us to do this next step.

Tip #2: Avoid negative self branding

"I'm ugly." "My nose is too big." "I suck at dinner dates." "I'm not a good speaker." These are just some examples of negative self branding. We make it a point to always hate something about ourselves. It may be our appearance, our sense of style, our abilities, and even our personalities. The question is, how better do you become when you convince yourself that you are no good? Should you not strive to improve yourself rather than completely degrade yourself? Learn to go past your inadequacies, and focus on how you will make yourself adequate or even how you will surpass adequacy. Break free from mediocrity! Laugh about your self-deprecations and work on improvements.

Tip #3: Appreciate your efforts

In most cases, people fail to give themselves a pat on the back. If we fall short of our dreams, then we feel as though we will never be good enough. I tell you: Stop! Life does not always give you lemons. Sometimes, you get a load of mud to work with. It is not to show you that mud is all you deserve. It is simply a natural rule of life that you will not always get what you want, and that sometimes your efforts mean more than your achievements. Give yourself a pat on the back. Trust me, it works.

Tip #4: Worrying kills

It is said that during calamities, more people die due to panicking than from the calamity itself. People are worry warts. We worry about those things that are beyond our control and believe that these are the things we are supposed to manipulate. Let us also keep in mind that our existence is bound by limitations, and that, at some point, something will always go against our plans. There are times when you just have to have a little faith.

Tip #5: Trust your abilities

You are more powerful than you might seem. And, no, I do not mean X-ray vision or invisibility. I mean that your mind is capable of conceiving great things and your body can always perform according to your state of mind. There have been reports that meditation has made it possible for a monk to levitate. In the same sense, if you believe in yourself and keep in mind that you are a powerful being, capable of achieving great things, then you will achieve great things. Believing in yourself will boost your morale and will definitely allow you to tap into that reservoir of physical and mental prowess.

Tip #6: Honesty is the best policy

In conceiving your desired realities, you also have to be honest with yourself. You are the author of your life, and any emotional detail must always be taken into account. People often ignore their feelings and prefer to live a life of numbness. This is not our nature. We are capable of feeling emotions, and we have to acknowledge these feelings. We have to take them into account because they play a huge role in our lives. These emotions are what separate us from animals. If we are happy, then we have to allow ourselves to feel that happiness. If we are sad, let us feel the sadness. Acknowledgement of these emotions, which play in our minds and hearts on a daily basis, will help us to determine how best to deal with and express them.

Tip #7: To err is human, to forgive is divine.

In life, you have to keep in mind that you will eventually make mistakes. If that day should come, do not be too hard on yourself. You cannot get all things right the first time. We all look at our mistakes as failures. I think differently. I say that you should look at your mistakes as steps on a stairway. If you want to go up, then you have to take it one step at a time or, in this case, one mistake at a time. You will begin to realize that having made a mistake has made you a wiser person, and that whatever mistakes you may have committed have not contributed to the deterioration of your self-esteem but to the improvement of future endeavours. Getting things wrong the first time means that you will get them right the next time around. Believe me, there are always second chances in life, learn to see them.

Tip #8: Reward yourself

Whenever you do a good job, treat yourself to a trip to the spa or the beach or some other place. You will not feel inspired to do better in your life if all you do is labour over work. There are times when you simply have to let yourself kick back for a while. These treats do not necessarily have to be expensive ones. It may even be as simple as having a pint of ice cream while watching a movie or a steak and beer night with friends. Whatever these treats may be, permit yourself to experience them every now and then. You deserve it.

These tips may be very small things, if taken literally. No matter how small and perhaps even insignificant they may seem, they have a noble purpose. These things will not only let you love yourself, but also look at yourself from a different, better perspective.

After reading these tips, do you feel the intense gusto to love yourself? Do you now see that you are an important part of yourself? Begin to internalize and apply these tips, and in no time at all, you will feel that you are constantly giving yourself a hug, an affirmation, and even a compliment. And no, these are not the workings of a crazy person.

Now that the personal aspect of love is dealt with, let us start to branch out into our surroundings. As we grow to have more love for ourselves day by day, we become like an overflowing pail of love. Time will come when we have no other choice but to share that love. We may share it with our loved ones, the people in the community, friends, significant others, even people who are a million miles away from us.

Regardless of the distance or the relation, it is important that the love we nurture inside is expressed, shown, given to and shared with others for it to be completely meaningful.

So, after discussing how we can love ourselves and others, it is now time to discuss how to love another aspect of life. Now, this aspect is quite a task to discuss, simply because it is highly significant in today's time. It is emotionally difficult, because I simply do not know how people may react to this, given that a lot of people may find that they can relate to this topic. And it is in this context that I am worried about how you will take this topic, as well as the justifications I have for it, because you may have your own objections to them. But I beg your indulgence, given that these are simply my experiences, and I wish to share them with you in hopes that they may prove themselves useful to you.

In the next pages, I shall be discussing how you can love your job. Now, a lot of people who are employed would tell you that they are simply employed for the purpose of survival and that they do not love their respective jobs. Because of economic difficulties, most people have been forced into jobs that are not of their preference, but are forced to take them because there are no other jobs available. This is when employment mismatching happens.

My tips will not solve employment mismatching. My tips will simply shed a small ray of hope for you. In turn, if these tips are put into action and if they change a person's viewpoint, I have changed the world one person at a time.

Read on and you will find out what I am talking about.

CHAPTER 3

LOVING YOUR JOB 101

It is easy to love your profession if it is in line with your interests or with what you took up in college. It is easy to adjust from being a student to being an employee, since we already have an idea of what we are going to do. That is not the case for many people. Most of them survive on a job that they do not like. Imagine living through your professional life as a person who is disinterested. This greatly affects your output as an employee, regardless of what output you are required to produce.

Seeing that this is a very widespread issue for most employed workers, I gave it some thought and decided that I would include it in this eBook. That way, if any of you, my dear readers, get to read this and relate your present situation to what I just mentioned, then I hope that I have your attention, because I wish to help you.

So, let us flip the pages and, together, we shall learn how to love our jobs and the way we work.

I have read numerous articles about how people can love their jobs. This chapter may prove to be just the same as all the others. The difference is that I am not somebody who is merely proposing tips; I am somebody who has put those tips into action. From all these nuggets of wisdom, given by resource speakers and authors of self-improvement books, I have gathered a few points that I think are the most important.

Tip #1: Keep in mind that your job is a constant and that you are the variable

The job may be filled by any other person than you. Lots of people are qualified to occupy that spot, but among the many others who applied for it, you were the one chosen to perform according to the tasks required of that position. That, in itself, is already something that you have to be proud of. You have to bear in mind that among all of them, you are the most qualified.

Tip #2: Remember that all jobs are created so that you may be of help to many other people

In whatever job you may have, always remember that that job was created so that you could be of service to your fellow men. That is the significance of your job. With each piece of paperwork you accomplish, with every request you approve, even with every passing hour of a boring shift, you are a benefit to society. You grant your services to a multitude of people, and you have to be happy that people see you as a benefit, not a liability. People tend to look for significance in the things that they do. And in this case, the significance you seek for is staring at you. Appreciate the job you have; I know many others do.

Tip #3: Your job is not only a means of survival

Very often, I come across people who tell me that they are working to survive. Although I think this is more an appeal to the government than oneself, I also believe that we are capable of seeing past that bitter reality. We go to work with a mindset that we work to survive. We seem to be no more than creatures in the wild who strive to survive. That is not a good implication. I have a better suggestion: Try to have a fresh and positive perspective. We must all try to look for something good in our jobs. This might be your coworkers, or your superiors, or even your subordinates; they are the ones who will give you a better perspective as to why you go to work. It will be like kindergarten, when even in the absence of a value for education, we are excited to go to school because we have friends there. That is what I propose.

Tip #4: Learn to save

Some people dislike their jobs because they do not seem to be making enough money. Let us consider this scenario: When people start working, they begin to have a concept of financial security. Since their first salary is not a big one, they find ways to make ends meet. Gradually, they are able to adjust, and eventually they do make ends meet even with their meagre salary. As the years of employment go by, people get raises and promotions, which also give them bigger salaries. The question is: What do people do with their raises? They spend it or pay more taxes.

That is the problem in that scenario. Whenever people get promoted, their expenditures are also promoted. It seems as though their expenditures are directly proportional to their raises.

Imagine the following scenario.

A person receives a salary of about $1,000 per month and is able to live on exactly $1,000 per month. If he gets a wage increase of another $100 per month and stays on his normal one thousand dollar expenditures, then he is able to save $100 every month. You may occasionally treat yourself to a few well earned rewards, but the thing is, you live within your means even if you get a raise.

Call me crazy, but I would rather have $100 in savings every month than a stack of notices for debt payments.

Tip #5: Love what you do so that you can do what you love

Your job is a way for you to learn to expand your horizons to more possibilities. I believe that, since you are earning money, you have the convenience of having something to take out of your wallet. In that case, if there are ever things that you desire to have, then you are able to gather your finances and acquire those things. And, no, I do not mean impulse buying. I mean wise spending. If you have always wanted to study painting, or music, or dancing, then having a steady income will eventually make that dream a reality. Your job is simply a means to fund those dreams of yours. In the long run, you will love your job, because it helps you do what you love to do. If that fails, then determine what you need to do to improve your situation, go back to school, think about moving on.

These are simple and rather radical ideas. They can be of help. Like all starters, these might seem to be quite difficult to accomplish at first. However, as you go along, you will find that they are effective and that they can help you appreciate your job, not only as a means of survival, but as a means to have fun.

I do not wish to exclude any group of people from this book, since I want my thoughts to go past age and qualifications. I would like to also appeal to the younger generation. Most of you may be idealistic, and all of you have that zest for life. I would like you to take heed of something very important: It is important to love education.

In today's world, even a college education is optional. Most of the teenagers prefer to find a job straight out of high school. My suggestion is that you learn to love education. Why? Because it is through education that you are able to ensure your future. If you have other dreams; that is fine, but never disregard the power of education. If everything else fails, at least you will have your fallback.

In this regard, I dedicate this part of the book to the youngsters, as I wish them to gather nuggets of wisdom from my experiences as well. I wish you, my young ones, to do a bit of soul seeking and self evaluation at this point in your life.

CHAPTER 4

LOVE FOR EDUCATION

In kindergarten, we all start out as bright eyed students eager to go to school. We do all sorts of things, and at the end of the day we tell our parents stories about school.

As we progress to a higher level of education, we begin to experience a lot of other things. We have the school bullies, the nerds, the musicians, the cool kids, the rich kids, the pretty ones, the hunky ones and all other groups. We may be part of one of those groups, or we may end up being solo performers. In any case, school becomes a bit more challenging. Elementary education is filled with much experimentation, and at some point or another we try some of them. And at the end of the day, all is well; moving on.

Then, we move up to middle school. Then, we have our first crush, some of us get our first kiss and more experimentation happens. New fashion trends spring out, bullies become worse, the rich kids remain rich, and the other groups undergo their own metamorphoses over time. Some of these changes are for the better, while some are for the worse. Still, school carries on, and for most kids becomes hell. At the end of the day, they wish school was over, but they still go to school the next day.

High school comes and, boy, does everything change again—relationships, cliques, puppy love, partying, drinking, prom and other things happen in a blur. It is at this point in your education that things change, and it is up to you where this change points to. Some wish to pursue their studies and move up to college. Athletes may go to schools that offer them athletic scholarships. Certain kids go on to the more intellectual type of scholarship and apply for grants to Harvard. Musicians seek out Juilliard. What happens to the rest of the kids? What happens to those kids who prefer to disappear in the background? This chapter is for you.

Your former classmates move on to college not only because of the scholarship. They have a dream, and they will eventually achieve it. Why? Because they tried. They make an effort to still go the extra mile after high school. I am not putting you down, nor do I look upon you as pitiful. In fact, I look upon everyone as a being with huge potential for greatness. I am no better than the others out there. I am taking the time to pause and talk to you, as many others talked to me when I was in my youth.

My young friends, school is not that bad. In fact, school is fun, especially college. You will learn a lot of things, and you will be able to get a glimpse of the future you wish to have. In most companies, college graduates trump non graduates on most occasions. If you wish to apply for a job, and you have a rival who has finished college, there is that big possibility that they will prefer him over you. A pleasing personality is good, but working requires a bit more than just personality. There has to be aptitude and competence. A college education will ensure that.

So, let's talk about college. What's so fun about it? And what will you expect when you prepare for college? Flip the page, and I will tell you.

The first question is: Why do I wish to talk to the youth of today about college? I have children of my own, and as a parent I want nothing but the best for them. I wanted them to value education because education will be their "bulletproof vest" in life. No matter what happens, as long as they have education, they will always have a fallback. Now, in what form will this "bulletproof vest" come? It is in the form of a college diploma.

Now, you tell me that a lot of successful people in the world did not even finish college or never even went to college. That is true. And they are successful indeed. This kind of success does not come to everybody. This happens only to a few and if that is so, are you certain that you are one of them? I say we do not know. So, how do we ensure success? Through EDUCATION and, more importantly, a college education.

Let us not rely on the possibility that you may be successful with just a high school diploma. Oh, sure, you can have part-time jobs and such. Was there not a time in your life when you wished to be something more? I am sure there was. And with a simple choice of going to college, you can have that dream in the palm of your hand and on a silver platter.

In some countries, students take up a certain major in college just because it is the trend, or because most of their friends are taking up that major as well. This may or may not be a good practice, and it is for this reason that I wish to caution the youth today. If you are going to pick out a course in college, I suggest that you do a lot of thinking first.

Now, the second question is: What do I need to think about? Allow me to enumerate:

1.   Think of what you want to do after college

You must have some sort of perceived future. Envision yourself a few years ahead and understand what you perceive in that vision. Do you see yourself as an engineer? A teacher? A doctor? A nurse? A soldier? A pilot? These are perceived futures for you. And these will help you think of what you want to become after you graduate. This points us to the number two.

2.   Choose a course that is directly or in some way related to your perceived future

You must remember that a relevant college education will give you better chances to land a job, especially the kind of job you wish to have. If you want to be a doctor, then you have to take up a medical direction, and then study medicine. Your learning has to match the application for which it is intended. In that case, working will be a piece of cake for you because you have learned much about it in college.

3. Always trust your heart

In any perceived future, you have to take your preferences and interests into consideration. A person who goes follows his preferences and abides by his interests will find that learning is easy. If you are more inclined to learn about food, then take up the Culinary Arts in chef school. Go towards your inclinations, and I assure you that school will be very easy, especially college.

4. Money may be a problem, but it is never an excuse

People say that they did not go to college due to financial constraints. So get a part time job and save your money to get you there. You were not the first financially deprived person and you would not be the last, but you have a choice and the choice is to take hold of the reigns. There are numerous scholarships from which you can choose. If you really wish to learn, then there is always a way. It is easier for somebody who wishes to learn but is financially constrained than it is for somebody who is well off but refuses to learn. Your mind is a powerful thing, and if you strive hard enough even you can make miracles come true.

5. Focus

College will be the time for ultimate independence and freedom. It is also at this time when a lot of you may start to flop. I say, focus. I say, reach your goals first. I say, persevere. It is a four year leg and a four year sprint for you. If you get distracted, like a horse on the road with no blinkers, then it will cost you dearly. So, once in college, persevere and endure. Focus and your efforts will pay off.

Now, the third question: Why do I claim that these are effective?

I have children, and had they not persevered, they would not be travelling the world now. They have the convenience of time and finances because they persisted and they focused on the goal. Now, they can be distracted all they want because they have all the time and the funds to spend.

If you wish to have the convenience of time and funds, then study hard and focus. It is worth it.

So, my young friends, I hope that you have picked up a few things from the tips I gave. These tips are given not to curtail your freedom to have fun and enjoy your lives, quite the contrary. I wish to cultivate that and enable you to have the time of your life when you grow old. If you do that at this point in your life, when preparation is needed, then you might miss out on your chance of having a sound future. So, work hard on your dreams and they will come true, for nothing is impossible.

Now that this chapter has come to a close, I do not wish to give you, the younger generation, the impression that you, my dear friends, will be excluded already. As you journey through this book, I hope that you, as well as the people who are more advanced in years, are able to gather wisdom from all I have to offer.

I invite you to read on, for the topics that follow concern you as well. You may find them to be of interest and relevance to you, so, please, turn the pages as well. But before that, ask me: What is next?

Read on and you will find out.

CHAPTER 5

TIME FOR ROMANCE

Now, this is a topic that I think almost everyone can relate to. I am now going to talk about the romantic type of love, or the kind of love shared between two people.

At a certain time, we all develop certain affection for other people. This type of affection develops into infatuation, and eventually we grow to love that person. I believe that it is always a process, and that love at first sight does also exist, perhaps that kind of love is much too physical and not visceral. To me, romance is a friendship that has undergone a facelift. And that is what I want to discuss in this chapter.

Now, people ask me how they are supposed to love their significant other, or how to express their love for a person they have fallen for. There are many ways to love and to express love. There are many ways by which that love is manifested through our actions and our words. I am not here to teach you what to say. I am here to discuss the whys and hows.

In this chapter, I will also be answering a few common questions about love. Note that these are merely opinions, and they may not be completely in agreement with the convictions of others.

So, let us begin.

What is love?

In the Bible, it says that love is patient, kind, not arrogant and does not look at the faults of others. Some would say that love is blind. Some would say that love is a battle. I believe that love is a synthesis of every single definition we know about it. Now, how do you synthesize the definitions? To me, love can be summarized in a few words: Love is a compromise.

Now, in what way is it considered a compromise? Love is not necessarily a tango, or a rumba, or any other dance you know. It takes two to tango but it only takes one person to dance. So, back to the question. In my opinion, love is a compromise because it requires that people meet somewhere in the middle. By that I mean that in a relationship, in any relationship, people must always try to meet halfway. Adjustments are necessary, as you journey together, because, as time goes by, you discover more and more things about the person you love. In that case, you must always be flexible, so that you ride the waves instead of fighting them.

Let us look at it from two points of view: the female and the male point of view. To a woman, it is important that the man she is with is sensitive, humorous, committed, and responsible. He must also be kind-hearted and respectful and must not forget their special days. A woman likes it if the guy goes with her during her shopping days and does not complain. She wants the guy not to slurp his soup or pasta, or to display 'manly manners' when she is around. That means no burping, no feet on the chair, and no cursing. To her, the best expression of love is shown through his actions. A woman likes it when the guy tells her that he loves her; a woman likes to be complimented; a woman wants to feel that she is the most special and the most beautiful woman to him. These are just simple gestures, but to women, these are priceless.

Now, let us take it from a guy's perspective. To a guy, simply saying it does the job. A friend of mine said to me once that men are born to become rocks. We are born into a status quo that men should be tough and should be "bulletproof" in a way. Our friends are constant reminders that we should not stray from that status quo, and that does it for us. We are subjected to the pressures of manhood, and it reaches a point where sensitivity becomes a sign of weakness. I do not mean to insult my group. In fact, I am proud to be a man. It just takes time before we open up. Women need to understand that some men prefer to watch sports and drink beer with their feet resting on the coffee table. Women also need to understand that, because we are immersed in our status quo for a long time, it will take some time before we get to adjust to the feeling of being soft. It is difficult for a guy to change his paradigm, simply because men stick to a certain system, and that is like a code for us.

To us men, love is similar to a rock fan going to a rock concert. We may start out with slow head banging and such. As the show progresses, we become hyped up. Although we are psyched to become rock hard inside, considering all the matching muscles that go along with it, there is a soft spot in us, and that is the spot that a woman occupies. Women can resist men, but no man can resist a woman. At some point, he will look for a woman to fill that soft spot. It may be a friend or a new significant other. Men are tough; but with the right woman, even the hardest of hearts will become mushy. Women have mastered that skill, the skill of making a man all muscle on the outside, but gooey inside.

So, these two genders have different perceptions about love. Women perceive it to be a fairytale type of love, while men are a bit more closed about it. This does not mean that there can be no common ground. You are bound to have common interests, and that is a good starting point. The question is: How do we do that?

Let us talk about that. How do we meet halfway?

As I have mentioned, love is a compromise; men and women need to meet halfway if they want their relationships to work. To me, this is very difficult to do. Why? Because arriving at a compromise means that we have to let go of things which we have been practicing since we were young. To women, it might be pride and security. To a man, it is the feeling of superiority. If both parties are willing to set those aside and come to an understanding, then things will become easy.

The following are some thoughts I have on love and relationships.

1. Segregate

I have a friend whose mother always tells him that women are princesses, and they must be treated as such. His father would also tell him that he can punch a guy in the face as hard as he can, and the guy will be okay with it; just do not crush his ego. These are examples of relationship killers. Pride, ego and the like. These come first in the wastebasket list. Next, determine the recycle list. Unearth your hidden qualities, which are helpful in keeping the relationship working, and recycle them. Reuse and reuse, as much as you can.

2. Both must talk, but both must listen also.

In relationships, both parties talk, and usually that's the only thing they do. As the woman is talking about her need to feel loved and all that, the guy is also screaming about something totally different. When this happens, an understanding is never really achieved. Come to think of it, if you record both parties and have their conversations played back to them, they will find that they seem foolish. They are fighting about one thing, but they are talking about different things. In a relationship, it is important that both parties should talk, but not at the same time. Both parties will get the chance to talk, and both parties will get the chance to listen. That is a must in any relationship. As you listen, do not put the person in prejudice. You must learn to listen and not just to hear them out. There is a difference between hearing and listening. Hearing is what happens when a sound is captured by your ear. Listening is when you pair that sound with rationalization and analysis. So, I say, listen to your significant other. They will not be complaining about something that is satisfactory to them. Surely, they have something to say, just as you do.

3. Determine your similarities or common interests, as well as your differences

I find that, for some people, keeping a list of their similarities and differences actually helps in maintaining a good relationship between them. If you both sit down and sort your interests according to similarities and differences, then it will be easier for you to work on a compromise. This helps in letting the two of you know which areas to enrich, which to maintain, and which to respect. Even if you are in a relationship, it is still best that you give each other breathing space. Allow each other to have time for yourselves, so that you won't get smothered. I say this even to married couples. Allow yourselves to just kick back and relax. Sometimes, when we go all out from the outset of a relationship, we end up getting burnt out. That is not good or healthy. So, give yourself a little private time. This may be going out with your friends for beer, or spending time with girlfriends on shopping sprees. Give yourselves time to miss each other, and I assure you that when you meet each other, it will seem like the first intense feeling of love rushing back in.

4. Try doing things together

I know that chick flicks are not a man's thing, in the same sense that testosterone packed mixed martial arts channels are not a woman's cup of tea. In most cases, there is only one television in the house, but two people who wish to watch something. I would like to say thanks to PVR and TiVo, but in this eBook, there is a principle involved. So, let us say there is or was no PVR or TiVo. What do you do when your favourite chick flick and the MMA championship round fall under the same timeslot? Honestly, a lot of people fight over such things, and relationships have been ruined because of that. Don't you think that it is a bit weird that you are willing to sacrifice your relationship just for a few hours of drama or punches and kicks? I say it is.

So, you both have to learn to respect each other's preferences and every once in a while start watching chick flicks with your wife or MMA with your husband, or at least pretend that you like it. It is important that are able to do stuff together, because a relationship, as I have mentioned, is a compromise. We cannot always have our way. And, no, the solution is not to buy another television set because, as I have said, there is a principle involved. If you buy another TV set, then you will be forced to watch TV separately, and as such the principle is lost.

So, try to kick back and enjoy each other's TV shows who knows, you might like them.

The tips I just gave are merely examples of how you are able to meet one another halfway. They are simply suggestions on how you will eventually find ways to formulate methods of your own. Now that we have discussed them, let us move on to other aspects. The next aspect which I would like to discuss is about love as a journey.

Similar to the journey we are in by reading this book, love is a journey in itself. Now, in what way is it a journey? We go from situation to situation, and we shift from one emotion to another, as well. In this journey, we have to understand that there are a lot of possibilities, and that we should anticipate them so that we are always prepared.

I hear women say that men are pigs. I hear men say that women are difficult. These are examples of an anticipated situation. But these are unhealthy anticipations, and they will not grant you a very harmonious relationship. In my opinion, we have to stop stereotyping each other. That is what I want to discuss in the next chapter.

So, once again, do read on.

CHAPTER 6

WEATHERING THE STORMS

In any relationship, things are always bound to happen. These may be good things or bad things. Like all other situations, we have to make sure that we are prepared to face them. In any battle, we have to make sure that we have the necessary weapons for us to last the war. According to a famous singer named Jordin Sparks, "Why does love always feel like a battlefield?" I agree with her. Love is a battlefield, and if you are not prepared, then you are bound to lose.

So, what kinds of preparations are we supposed to make? It is important that we learn all about love. Love is, in itself, a very complicated topic, and the only thing we must expect is the unexpected. Sometimes, people would even consider falling in love as coincidental. In that case, there are many things to put into consideration.

First, being in a relationship will always require time. If you wish to be in a relationship with any person, be it a friendly or romantic one, that relationship will always require that you allot a portion of your 24 hours strictly to it. One cannot imagine making a relationship last without having the time for it. Lots of relationships have fallen because of the shortage or even absence of time.

Second, love has its accompanying heartaches. They say that love is pain, and pain is love. True enough, love means that one is willing to go through pain. Because of our imperfect natures, we are bound to hurt each other's feelings at some point. If we are to engage in a relationship, we have to anticipate that we will eventually get hurt, and it is in that anticipation that we are able to gauge if we truly love the person or not. If you are willing to go through all that disappointment just to be able to spend time with the person you love, then that is love.

Third, love will always have its reasons. You should always remember why you love the person. You need to remember this, so that when all things fail, you know why you are in that situation in the first place. It is important because, as you go along your journey, a time will come when everything will turn cold and routine like. It is during these moments that people want reasons. Should that happen to you, you will now have your reasons.

Lastly, love will always find its way. And, no, my friends, this is not an act of desperation. If you love somebody, you will always find a way to let him or her know how much you love them. I do not mean that you have to just go out and tell them. There are things to consider when you wish to express your feelings. If the love cannot be returned to you, then accept this fact. If you are truly meant to be together, then you will be. That is a natural law of life. Looking for ways does not mean that you have to look for opportunities where your loved one will fall into your hands. It is imperative that you let love find a way for you, and not the other way around.

These little things mean so much when we put them into action. These little things determine how happy and fulfilled we will be in our relationships, because despite the simplicity of these realities, they are the ones which are of much significance to us. Moreover, these are the little things we usually forget in our emotional dealings with other people, and even with ourselves. So, before we begin to love our way through life, let us stop and think and always believe that love is ever powerful.

My friends, we are done talking about love. We have gone from the love inside of us to reaching out to others through our love for them. We have gone from one advice to another, and I hope that, as you followed the path I have drawn up for you, you were able to get a glimpse of how these tips may improve your relations with other people.

The advice and thoughts which I have included in this chapter are no more than tips, but as you put them into action and application, I believe that they can become more than just words. They will become bridges not towards places, but towards people.

I would like to end this chapter with a quote from Friedrich Nietzsche:

"There is always some madness in love. There is also always some reason in madness."

As I thought about what to write in this book, I also thought about how to make its parts interconnected. As you may have noticed, I love to take a breather and just ask you how your journey was. I also try to let you visualize how the previous topics have some sort of relevance in the topics that follow. After this chapter, I was supposed to write about something else entirely, and I figured that if I do so, I might lose the flavour of this book. So, I pondered on it for a few days and came to a conclusion that I need to add another chapter. Now, what could be a good topic to follow after love? I believe that there could be no better topic than happiness.

So the question is: Why happiness? I guess it's because you can never really talk about love without eventually touching the topic of happiness. In fact, you cannot talk about happiness without somehow relating it to your experiences of love. So, as these things unfold on a daily basis, I would like to discuss them in this chapter. And no, not just the happiness we get from love, but happiness as a whole. Where do we find our happiness? What makes us happy? These questions will be answered if you read on.

PART 5

HAPPINESS

"If you want to be happy, be."

~Leo Tolstoy

I guess the big question now is: How can we be happy? We daydream many times during the day. We dream about virtually anything, but most of all, we dream about the things that bring us satisfaction and happiness. We dream about that sports car we saw yesterday, we dream about that house we have always wanted to buy, that dream vacation, that big promotion, that fat paycheque and, basically, anything under the sun. As with all dreams, we wake up and they are gone. In truth, our dreams stay dreams, and happiness becomes elusive once again.

Do not think you are reading the wrong chapter. Yes, I am talking about happiness. So, what is happiness and how can we achieve it? According to my sources, happiness is a state of mental well-being. This state may be interpreted according to the different aspects of society. Not one of them shares a common definition, except maybe that it is a state of joy.

CHAPTER 1

HOW TO BE HAPPY

Happiness is ephemeral, subject to the vagaries of everything, from the weather to the size of your bank account.

I am not suggesting that you can reach a permanent state called "happiness" and remain there. There are many ways to swerve off the path of anxiety, anger, frustration and sadness into a state of happiness once or even several times throughout the day. Here are some ideas to get you started. Choose the ones that work for you. If tuning out the news or making lists serves only to stress you further, try another approach.

1. Appreciate the simple things in life
2. Enjoy the fresh air, the morning cup of coffee or tea
3. Say "hello" to your neighbours
4. Walk your pet, give it some hugs
5. Count your little blessings and appreciate that you are alive
6. Smile at a stranger
7. Give something of yourself to a needy person
8. Read an uplifting article or book
9. Exercise and eat well
10. Love yourself and do something special
11. Last of all, say thank you to the creator

These are just a few examples that I find to be very helpful, even to me. As much as we are diverse and varied in nature, we are alike in our quest for happiness. Nobody wants to live a life of loneliness. At some point, each of us wants to smile and laugh with people. It is in these simple acts that we can be sure that we are in pursuit of happiness.

Speaking about pursuits of happiness, have you watched the movie starring Will Smith entitled *The Pursuit of Happyness*? I believe that it shows a perfect example of how people struggle to find happiness and purpose in their lives. Mr. Gardner, the main character, had a beautiful wife and a son. He was a salesman, but things were not working out for him; his wife in the end left him; he had to struggle to mind his son, often sleeping in shelters, on the streets, in the subway washroom.

Then one day he said that he could no longer live like this. He decided that he had to change the direction of his life. What did he do? He decided that poverty is something that is not pleasant, so he decided that he would commit to becoming a stockbroker but in so doing he had to overcome many, many obstacles, such as lack of food, no taxi fares, no job, even spent a day in cell for not paying his parking tickets. He was penniless; he could not pay his bills, even mere rent. To cut a long story short, he moved on to become the best in his business, the richest man in his firm and earned all the money he had ever wanted.

The question is: Is Mr. Gardner happy? Let us try to find out. Imagine yourself in the shoes of Mr. Gardner. Imagine yourself stuck in a rut which you cannot seem to get out of. Imagine sleeping inside a shelter with your son. Then imagine being the top broker in your company and the richest one as well. Now, tell me, would you be happy? Of course, you would be!

Mr. Gardner is no superhuman life form. He is a person; a human being, just like you and I and if Mr. Gardner was reading this now, I bet he would agree with me on this. He has no x-ray vision or super strength. He had a dream, and he went for it. And now, he is happy.

Because of this, the next chapter will be fully about happiness and your dreams.

CHAPTER 2

HAPPINESS AND DREAMS

I think that the story of Mr. Gardner can shed some light on the rather gloomy subject of happiness and success. From his story, it would seem as though he became happy because he was successful. While it may be a much-known fact that most successful people are happy, we also have to consider that that is not the only scenario to recognize.

I do not know whether many others have given it some thought, but I think that *The Pursuit of Happyness* was given the most appropriate title. Why? Because it was his pursuit of happiness that led him to becoming successful. So you see, it was not just his success that made him happy; it was also his eagerness to become happy. This is much like Tolstoy's statement that if you want to be happy, then *be* happy, although Mr. Gardner found his happiness by pursuing it. Still, it was happiness that fuelled his determination to be happy. It became an inspiration, a motivation in itself, and that is what I would want you all to do, my friends. Make your happiness your inspiration and your motivation. Fuel your drive to become happy and to find that happiness, and I assure you, you will be successful.

So, what's next? Let's talk about treasuring moments. In most cases, happiness is only temporary. Eventually, people will become sad, and eventually, people will forget that they are happy. And that, my friends, is not good. Happiness goes away because we choose to let it go. We choose to not feel it anymore, and we choose to let our tribulations take over.

So, let us count the ways to make all these go away. Let us count the ways of treasuring that happiness and making it last a very, very long time. Read on, friends.

CHAPTER 3

CHERISH THOSE MOMENTS

Tip #1: Know that happy moments do not last forever

It is in our nature that if we know something is bound to disappear, we savour each moment of it. That goes for our happiness, too. If we only keep in mind that eventually we will feel sadness again, then we may just hold onto those happy feelings quite a bit longer.

Tip #2: Think of the sad moments you have had in your life

Once we know what we have gone through just to become happy, we will know just how valuable those happy moments are. I bet Mr. Gardner never forgot his experiences; the ones that have made him successful. I bet that thinking of those struggles will make his happy moments all the more sweet.

Tip #3: Allow yourself to fully experience happiness

When happy moments occur in your life, do not be detached from them. Some people just acknowledge those happy moments, but they are not completely into them. My suggestion is, take part in those moments so that you will know the beauty of feeling happiness and being happy.

Tip #4: Always keep in mind that happiness is a reward, a blessing and not merely a stroke of luck

You have to remember that you are happy for a reason. You are happy because something made you happy. Do not look upon your happiness as just a product of sheer luck. Happiness is a gift, and not a lottery result. Your happiness is a product of what you have done and what you have made. So, feel proud and know that you are the author of your happiness.

Tip #5: Happiness is a weapon

When you are happy, you have weapons to use against sadness. You may ask me: In what way? Think of it this way: Whenever you feel sad or lonesome, you can always think happy thoughts, like Peter Pan. He is a perfect example that thinking happy thoughts will make you fly albeit not literally. It will give you that uplifting you need, and what's more, you get to stay young. Try it, it works like magic!

So, friends, I hope that you have been able to gain some nuggets of wisdom from this chapter. Happiness is a good thing, and there is no such thing as "too happy." There is just that sublime feeling of happiness, which we are all entitled to feel and savour. If you ask me, feeling happy once in a while can actually save a life. Lots of people take their own lives due to depression, and I feel that they are the ones who have had no reason to become happy, or if they have had that reason, they have not found a way to make that reason a reality.

Lots of us go through this world complaining about a lot of things; I suggest that we all try to become fruitful, in a way. Let us try to simply be happy that we are alive and that life is a means for us to achieve the things that we want. A woman I once knew always told me that, as long as there is one breath of life in you, then there is always a chance that you can make your dreams come true. I agree and that is the same thing I want you to remember.

I hope that you have learned a lot from this chapter. It only has a few pages, since I made it a point to compress the details, simply because these are the ones which are most pertinent. Do not worry; we still have a lot of things to discuss in the next few chapters. So, once again, I invite you to read on.

PART 6

MONEY

In life, there are certain things that we would love to get our hands on, and among those, I believe that money is at the top of the list. I would surely like some, and I am sure all of you would, too. Despite this desire to earn or simply have money, many people would say that money is the root of all evil. It is not!

It is for that reason that I wish to discuss money matters in this part of the book. I wish to shed some light on the topic. We all want to have money, and lots of it. We have to know what principles are involved when we discuss financial subjects.

Do not worry; I will not be lecturing you on how to save and all that. I will simply talk about money and how we should perceive money in our lives. So, if money is important, and if you wish to learn more about it, then read on.

Money seems to be a very, very important topic nowadays. People seem to be in a fuss when money is the topic. The question is: Why? Well, yes, I do acknowledge that money is very vital, because it is what we use to purchase our needs. We can love it, hate it, or worship it. Most people would probably spend it, but I'd define it. What is so important about it?

Let us view money from a very general aspect. First of all, it is a vital component of society because it is a means by which we are able to purchase our needs and wants. How do we attach value to something that is already a standard of value itself? How, then, do we measure the value of money besides the indicators of its value written on it? What makes it tick?

Money is measured not only by its value, but also by the importance we give to it. We love money. We worship it, and we would do virtually anything to have it. That, my friends, is the very expression of its value. And that is the reason why it makes the world go round; because we allow it to. For many of us, money is our life's remote control. We operate according to the edicts of our financial status. If we are rich, we splurge and spend and invest. If we are poor, our expenditures are limited.

So, let us dig deeper and discover more about money . . .

CHAPTER 1

MONEY: A DEFINITION

Money, by definition, is any object or record that is generally accepted as payment for goods and services. The main functions of money are distinguished as: a medium of exchange, a unit of account, a store of value and, occasionally in the past, a standard of deferred payment. Any kind of object or secure verifiable record that fulfills these functions can serve as just one definition among many. In society, this is our understanding of money. We term it as an object of value. Let us not focus on the word *object*, but on the word *value*.

If you look at it, that dollar bill you hold in your hand is not even a piece of paper. Paper bills are actually made out of a number of different fibres including plastic. Now, I am not trying to act all smart. This is just an example of how we are ignorant about it. We handle money daily. We use it to buy food, to go shopping, to pay for our fare and for any other financial transaction we may have. When asked, we do not even know what it is made of. Sure, we are certain that money is of value, but because we are so attached to what it means to us, we do not even know its components.

That is what is different with society nowadays. We seem to always ignore the little stuff because we are more concerned with the bigger picture. Our mental projections can never accommodate both the bigger picture and the little details.

So, let us begin our journey.

Without money, you will not be able to survive for very long unless you have a great-aunt, uncle, or other relative to support you. 99.99 per cent of the people who live in this world need money to survive because money is the currency that evaluates our wealth and our standards of living.

I say these things because that is what you always hear from people. *"Oh, I have no more money! How will I survive?"* Let us imagine how people survived millenniums ago. They did not have any form of currency in the past. They contented themselves with hunting and whatnot. I am not telling you to go hunting. I am telling you that if people in the past acted and thought the way we do now, humankind would have died out many centuries ago.

What values do you have in your life? What are the most important things in your life? As you grow older, your value system changes, so does your knowledge, but at the very beginning of life, I am sure your parents told you about the things you should not do; what is right and wrong. So, when you do something, your natural instinct goes into gear and tells you whether what you are doing is right or wrong. When this happens, your values start showing up, and you either do it or you do not. Your conscience is your guide, and it does this daily, guiding you throughout the day. But sometimes we ignore it and get into trouble. Our guidance system is our intuition; it tells you when you go wrong. And then you need to adjust your behaviour pattern in order to get back on course.

I guess that it is safe to say that we are all guilty of this crime. Let us also consider the other things that are vital to us. Money is not everything in this world. Some of us learn that the easy way, and some learn the hard way. No matter the intensity, what is important is that you learned.

So, if money is more than just something of value, then what is it? In my opinion, money is also something of principle. Why do I say this? Because, first of all, it takes principle to be able to handle it well. People say that money is the root of all evil. Why do we place the blame on something inanimate? My friends, money is not the root of evil we are!

I say this with complete confidence because I know that money cannot decide for itself, but people can. We are all very much into the concept of accumulating as much money as we can by whatever means, and that is where greed starts. My friends, money is not the problem. It is our greed that makes things go bad. It is our greedy nature that transforms money from a standard of trade to a standard of inequality.

So, how do we avoid all these? Let us count the ways . . .

Tip #1: Be content

It seems that everywhere we go, there are always new things to have: Cell phones, iPads, laptops, cars, and various types of gadgets. Each one of these is another reason for us to feel that we need more money. What we do not realize is that the phone we have now and the phone that just got released performs the same basic function: sending text messages and communicating with people.

For us to be content, we must realize that all phones are similar, except for some features.

Tip #2: Be thankful for the basics in life

We are all very concerned about fashion, technology and innovations. We get facelifts, bigger muscles, cooler hairstyles, more expensive clothes and all that. But have we stopped to think about how many others in the world do not even have a decent place to sleep or clothes to wear? We should stop being so vain and materialistic. We should try to think about those people, and stop and be thankful that we have the things that we have in life. Because what we do not realize is that somewhere out there a kid, a family, or a whole village is in dire need.

Tip #3: Wants or needs?

It is a known fact that we all have a thin distinction between these two. Most of us equate our wants to needs, simply because we follow only a certain pattern of thinking. Whatever catches our fancy also catches our desires. We always end up needing the things we want, because we create reasons for them to be of importance. This is the root of greed. We have to remember that our wants can always be acquired at some point in time. We do not need to have them right away. So, if there is an insufficient supply of money, then do not force yourself to try and afford everything.

Tip #4: Again, be content

A poet once wrote, "As a rule, man is a fool. When it's hot, he wants it cool. And when it's cool, he wants it hot, always wanting what is not."

This is a reminder of how fickle man is. This fickle nature drives us to swing from one principle to another, depending on what suits us. We can never be satisfied with just a single set of principles. If this is the case, then how can we expect to be satisfied with just a given amount of money?

Our contentment is what opposes greed. If we all become content with what we have, financially speaking, then there will be no reason for people to steal or rob. Corruption would become a thing of the past, and we can be sure that nobody is trying to win over another. These are small ways, but they are sure ways to battle greed and get rid of our monetary stereotypes. Break free!

So, enough about greed. Let us look at the significance of money in society, according to the viewpoints of numerous people. These I would like to quote, because I feel that this is how people define money.

"Money," wrote Ayn Rand, cult author and controversial profounder of objectivist philosophy, "is a tool of exchange, which can't exist unless there are goods produced and men able to produce them. Money is the material shape of the principle that men who wish to deal with one another must deal by trade and give value for value."

This is a very simple definition of money as a tool by which services or goods are compensated for. Let us look at other definitions of money which hold a kind of philosophy behind them.

CHAPTER 2

THE EVILS OF MONEY

"The man who damns money has obtained it dishonorably;
the man who respects it has earned it."

~Ayn Rand

Now, this is something that we can all comment on. I believe that corruption is already a big issue nowadays, and it is almost always attributed to money. Is money really the core of corruption? As I mentioned a while ago, money is never the root of evil, or corruption for that matter, because it is inanimate. *We* are the root of all evil, because we are the ones who are able to feel that greed and lust for wealth.

We have fallen as slaves to this monetary figure, instead of us enslaving it. We allow ourselves to be consumed by it, instead of us consuming its value. How can we permit ourselves to fully depend on our financial status? We think of poverty as living death, but why? Poverty is not the absence of money, but the absence of the means. People are not poor because they do not have money. People are poor because they do not have the means to earn that money. If beggars can go out on the street and earn a few bucks, then I believe we can be smart enough to think of ways.

So, I will discuss this in the next few pages. We will talk about salaries and earnings.

CHAPTER 3

LIVE WITHIN YOUR MEANS

What does it mean to live within your means?

Living within your means is not going overboard with your spending. For me, it is important that we should all remember our first salary. That first salary is a perfect example of living within our means. We make a budget to fit the salary that we have. At least this applies to the majority of us who receive a small amount.

As your salary begins to increase, your expenditures also tend to increase. And this is what I wish to point out. Imagine the savings you will have by just saving your wage increase and still living within the budget! I will show you how you can save up and retire early!

- You do not always have to go for the signature brands. Buy the store brands instead. The store brands may not be as popular, but at least they are not too particular in terms of washing and pressing. Truth is, you can save more money with the store brands because you do not have to send those to professional cleaners; you can clean them yourself!

- Refrain from always stopping by fast food chains. Not only do these places serve unhealthy food, they are also heavy on the budget. You can still eat out when you want, but try not to pay them a visit too often. You can do it once a week, but not every day. It will be lighter on your belly and on your pocket.

- Shop at you-bag-it supermarkets. When you are not subsidizing a store's deli section, flower shop or bakery, you will find the rest of the food cheaper. No frills supermarkets cut overheads by having fewer employees, smaller buildings to heat and cool, and by selling primarily store brands. You will quickly notice the savings.

- Instead of stopping by fast food chains, try to bring a packed lunch to work or school. It is economical, and it still fills your stomach. It also helps you lose weight, because fast food meals are packed and processed with preservatives and oils, making them unhealthy. So, try the brown bag and see your savings increase.

- Use coupons, but be smart about it. When a brand name product still costs more than a store brand, even after the deduction with a coupon, it not a bargain. Most coupons are for new products companies want you to try, so be selective.

- Buy used instead of new books; they are cheaper. Go to the local library if there is one in your community or village.

- Keep your car as long as you can afford it. A shiny new car may impress your family and friends, but it simply costs too much. It is just a matter of taking care of your car. Live within your budget.

- If you own a credit card, then try not to use it unnecessarily. Pay in cash. Why? Because cash payments do not have interest rates. If possible, try to save up for the things you want instead of using your credit card. I believe there is a perfectly good reason why they call it such.

- Reward yourself for your efforts. Your goal is to be frugal, not a miser. Small rewards, within your budget, are a wise way to add fun into your life. Living beneath your means takes self-control, but the emotional and financial benefits are tremendous. An occasional treat energizes you to keep up the good work.

The tips I have provided are not difficult to develop. But I tell you, the moment you begin to develop this routine, you will find that they are very effective in cutting down expenditures and increasing your savings!

Now we are done with money value. It is time to discuss the ways to value a person in terms of money. I will now answer the question: Who is the boss: Money or emotions?

CHAPTER 4

WHO IS THE BOSS?

In truth, ladies and gentlemen, money was made as an exchange medium for goods and services. It was created so that there would be equality in trade and business. Because commerce was beginning to expand in ancient times, they decided that trading would not be such a fair system for this expanding aspect of society.

Let us not forget that money was invented to serve man's purpose and that is equality. Let us not shy away from this thought. Money was created so that people would have a clear understanding of business, and not so that people could have a reason to become bearers of avarice. We are civilized people, and because of this we should exude civility. Corruption is not a sign of a civilized man.

There is still one thing to discuss, and that is how to value your money. We all know that money is important. Do we see it as important because it is, or because we need it? Do we have reasons why we value our money?

It is time for us to determine the right reasons for valuing money, given that a lot of people have forgotten them. Trust me, as I am writing this, I am doing a bit of soul-searching myself. I am starting to discover more about my life as I try to let you discover more about yours.

So, dear readers, join me and let us discover more about ourselves as we proceed to the next chapter.

CHAPTER 5

MONEY AND ALL THE RIGHT REASONS

Why do we value money?

First, because of the value system attached to it. The more money you have, the more comfortable your life is.

Second, it gives us the pleasure of acquiring our needs, because it is through money that we purchase our groceries and other pertinent items.

Third, it is because money will buy you almost anything. I hate to admit it, but for most people, this third choice is the priority one.

The question now is: Is that all?

Friends, we have lost sight of our values because we prefer to focus on the values of other things. Instead of looking at our own values, we give more attention to the value of money. Some people lose their sanity over money and some go berserk. People become so twisted up in this matter, but nothing good seems to amount from it.

I see it differently. I think that people need to be reminded as to why they should value their money. Philanthropy is not my forte, but it is definitely my topic.

All around the world, millions of people are dying because of poverty and hunger. It is estimated that the rich people of this earth take up almost 70 per cent of the world's resources, while they only comprise about 20-30 per cent of the population. The other 70-80 per cent thrives on the remaining 30 per cent of the world's resources.

Imagine, with all that money in the world, we still cannot solve hunger and poverty. For those who have money, the sight of all those poor people is heartbreaking, but it does not change how they value money. So, if we are to value money, let us value it for the right reasons.

These reasons, which I will be providing, will help give people a glimpse of just how important their wealth is and ensure that they value it for the right reasons.

So read on . . .

Reason #1: Money is neither planted nor harvested

Let us keep in mind that the money we have is a product of our hard work. We should always think of how much we have toiled to earn that sum of money. As much as your expenditures are your own business, it is, however, a must that you have a think about whether your efforts are worth it.

Reason #2: You will not be working forever

Well, yes, you may or may not have a pension. Do you really want to live your life according to what your pension can afford for you? Or would you like to save up for a rainy day? While you are still earning, take a part of your salary, approximately 10%, and put it in your savings. If invested wisely through your banks or credit unions, you will have substantial savings come retirement age. I know it is difficult to save in the present day, but at least put away a few dollars from each paycheque. I remember my mom special piggy bank. She made slots in a bamboo pole and there she would drop coins in it.

Reason #3: You do not have to beg for money on the streets or forage for food in garbage cans

Yes, you are lucky because you have a job and you are earning an honest salary. I doubt that you would want to live, even for a day, in the shoes of those people who are hungry because you do not want to give up a life of luxury and convenience. So, I suggest that you spend wisely.

These are simple tips. They are doable, and I believe that you wish to always live a comfortable life. I want that, too. And since it has always been my dream to impart knowledge to other people, I am doing it now. I am imparting knowledge to you so that you, like me, can learn about life.

Speaking about life, there is one more topic left, and it is a very big aspect of our lives. Maybe for some it is no longer an issue because they prefer not to have one. For those who do, and even for those who do not, the following is an important topic.

We are going to discuss religion.

PART 7

RELIGION

"Religion is the opium of the people."

~Karl Marx

The question is: Why did Karl Marx stand by his conviction that religion is the opium of the people? Religion may or may not calm our nerves; it does not enhance any physical strength or functions; it does not take away chronic pain. It does not exist in the form of pills, serums, powders or whatnot. I believe that Karl Marx observed a certain trait of religion, and his conclusions are founded, basically, on the perceived truth during his time. For me to be able to justify my stand, let us try to look at this from a scientific point of view.

Opium is an addictive narcotic drug which is extracted from the latex excretions of the opium poppy seed pod. This particular substance contains a significant amount of morphine and alkaloids, some of which are used in manufacturing heroin. In this sense, opium, thanks to its morphine content, functions most likely as a painkiller. Furthermore, the presence of certain alkaloids used in the production of heroin also makes it a downer. Being an opiate itself, it has a rather euphoric effect. How is this related to religion?

In the past, people had a high regard for religion. It was so high that during those times, the church and the state were one; whatever problem either one faced, one was sure that the other would come to the rescue. The people took refuge in one or the other, although it appears that the church became the more popular choice. Politics looked upon people as citizens, but the church considered them family members. The church offered words of consolation to the downtrodden. The church gave hope to those who needed it, and the church served as a home for those who sought shelter.

From this, we may see why Karl Marx considers religion an opiate. It provides relief to the soul, which has been beaten and bruised by countless adversities. It allows the person to feel calm, relaxed, as though in euphoria, and most of all, it allows the person's heart to rest, just until the effect wears off and another adversity will try and batter down that heart.

So, my dear friends, if your heart, your soul, or your mind needs to vent out and rest, say a little personal prayer. It's the little pill that will make your boo-boos go away.

What is the importance of religion? The writer is anonymous

I have found this article about this very question. These reasons are good because they are ecumenical, in a sense. I would like to share the article with you, and I hope that you will read it through.

In Sociology, the word *religion* is used in a wider sense than when it is used in religious books. Thus some sociologists define religion as those institutionalized system of beliefs, symbols, values that provide groups of men with solution to the question of ultimate meaning. Though religion is a highly personal thing, it has a social aspect and social role to play. It has been a powerful agency in society and performs many important social functions. According to A. Green, religion has three universal functions. These are:

(1) Religion explains individual suffering

Man does not live by knowledge alone. He is an emotional creature. Religion serves to the emotions of man in times of his sufferings and disappointment. On God religion puts faith and entertains the belief that some unseen power moves in mysterious ways to make even his loss meaningful. In this way religion gives release from sorrow and release from fear. It helps man to bear his frustration and integrate his personality.

(2) Religion enhances self importance

Religion expands one's self to infinite proportions. Man unites himself with the Infinite and feels ennobled. Society also gains from the self flattery provided by religious belief. Religion assures a greater reward in the afterlife to worldly failures than to successful life. Such kind of assurance encourages members to continue to play their part in society.

(3) Religion acts as a source of social cohesion

Religion is the ultimate source of social cohesion. The primary requirement of society is the possession of social values by which individuals control the actions of self and others and through which society is perpetuated. Science and technology cannot create this value. Religion is the foundation upon which these values rest. "Children should obey their parents, should not tell lies, women should be faithful to men, people should be honest and virtuous" are some of the social values which maintain social cohesion.

(4) Religion encourages social welfare

Religion has also performed some other services to humanity, such as the provision of work, the priesthood often dedicated to art and culture. The priesthood lays the foundation of medicine. It also fulfils the functions of scholars and scientists. Religion has served humanity through spreading education and also creating the habit of charity among the people, who open many charitable institutions such as hospitals, rest houses, and temples, as well as working to help the poor.

(5) Religion is the agency of social control

Religion provides a model for living. It upholds certain ideals and values. The believer imbibes these ideals and values in his life. Religion can help youth generation to become moral, disciplined, and socialized citizens of society.

(6) Religion controls economic life.

Max Weber was of the view that religion also controls economic life. To Weber, capitalism grew in the Protestant nations such as England and the United States of America. It did not grow in Italy and Spain where the people are Catholic. The Hindus place great emphasis on spiritual progress as opposed to material progress. Hence, materialism could not grow in India.

In this chapter, I would like to deviate from the normal terms with which religion is discussed. We are going to turn our heads from the generally accepted truths about religion so that we may focus on our perspectives.

What is your religious type? I did not mean to ask, because it does not matter. Religion, my friends, is not an edict. It is not something given to us by leaders who stand and declare that they have been chosen among many to lead. No, I believe that religion extends farther than just the embodied presence of an *ultimate being*. I believe that religion is a personal choice, and that religion is always a personal matter.

We believe that we are less justified than our leaders, because we believe that they have fewer tendencies towards errors. They are just like us, in every human way possible. Sure, some went through religious studies, others not, but remember, my friends, that they are no better than the people they preach to.

God never created religion, wealth or poverty. Men, Kings and Queens have created religion to suit their needs and to create obedience by the masses, and we have been told this from time to time but we never listened. Without thinking, we believe in what our parents, our religious leaders say. Where did they get their information from? Ask your leaders about what they were before they became "religious". Please ask questions about "GOD". When we were children growing up, no one ask questions of our pundits and gurus, if you ask questions that was mind provoking, either your parents or holy masters looked at you differently. And so we believe without questioning the rationale and truth about what our religious leaders told us and so we pass this information to our children and grand children. Time is in motion; children are by far more intelligent than our olden days. In the name of God and religion, we fight with each other daily; we have in many ways become more ignorant to the truth. In fact, the simple truth is you do not need to pray to a God if you do not want to, whether you pray or do not pray it makes no difference in the larger scheme of the universe, one gets results from knowledge, hard work, kindness and self-confidence and not from praying to "God". Let us test this simple premise, two children want to attend university, one is a believer in God, prays more than he studies, the other does not pray but understands the tasks at hand, prepares, works hard, take extra lessons, parties when needed, enjoys life, and is very consistent and focused. Please tell me which have the greater probability of getting into university? You have the answer my friends.

When people talk about religion, it is unavoidable that they also mention faith. What is faith, and how does it contribute to success?

According to a writer, Quang Van, faith is important in any endeavour. Now, you may ask me why. For starters, people who believe in what they do have better chances of achieving their dreams compared to those who do not. When talking about success in terms of faith, both religion and science will agree on this. In addition to this, Quang Van expounds by citing a scientific reality called the RAS, or the Reticular Activation System. This phenomenon is best explained that when people wish to do or achieve something, they are most likely to notice TV shows, magazines, or articles related to that endeavour.

For example, when you are into DIY (do-it-yourself), you are most likely to tune in to DIY tv shows or purchase DIY magazines, simply because they appeal to you as something vital in the achievement of your dream or the fulfillment of a project.

Another example would be the recuperation period following surgery. Most people who watch comedy shows tend to heal faster than those who do not watch comedy shows. It is their faith that allows them to achieve their goals faster.

With this mentioned, I now ask you a question: How do religious leaders fall into place?

We do not owe the achievement of our dreams to the dictates of religious leaders. Their proclamations are not measures of success, because your success will only be determined by your willingness to realize that dream and hard work.

You have the power within you to create your own world. Remember that when you were a child, you copied everything you saw, and then you did what your instincts told you were the right thing to do. Create your own world, dream big, commit to your dream and work every day at it and it will happen.

So, now that we are quite acquainted with religion, let us discuss a few other aspects of it. First, let us explore generosity.

Numerous religions have their own understanding of generosity. For some, it is the textbook version, which is simply giving; and for others, it is the rendering of services to people. Yet others would pertain to it as a form of charity and the list goes on. I wish to tackle just a bit about it, since I do not want to claim that I am in any way an expert in the world's religions.

We will only be focusing on the general definition of generosity, which is giving. So, let us begin.

CHAPTER 1

GIVING

My mother always said that the more you give, the more you receive in return. I did not know how it was possible. Here is the magic: When you give to people less fortunate than yourself, you receive blessings unknown to you. The universe reacts by rewarding you for your efforts, so that you are able to continue giving.

So universally, the laws work with you, not against you. It is like trying something for the first time. At the beginning, you do not know how to get it done, but then you receive a tremendous amount of help from people you do not know, and the project is completed before you know it. It is just like me starting to write this book; I did not have any means of getting this done, but the ideas and images just kept flowing. And I do hope that people will get something out of the lessons and the stories I tell. I truly mean that, because you all deserve better, and if you learn from the lessons then it will happen to you. I am blessed with whatever I have, and I am grateful to the Universe for its blessings; I am not wealthy but blessed with great family and friends.

Today something came to my mind, and it triggered a sentiment from many years ago, when I was a young boy growing up. It dawned on me that as we age, we start remembering things that happened to us when we were children growing up. I remembered the fun times with my mother and father, which brought back beautiful memories. Even though we had very little in life, we were very happy as children growing up with my siblings.

I cherish those memories, as my siblings all got married and now we have all ventured off along different paths in life. We created new families and new circles but family is always precious in every way. We should always keep contact with our family on a regular basis, because life is short and we do not have much time before we are all gone and all that remains to treasure are the memories of our dear ones.

So, now your job is to do what is best for you; tell your family that you care for them and that you are happy to have them as part of your own.

How Giving Can Help You

Ever notice that those who are truly very wealthy and successful are always involved in charities? Many of them are not just writing cheques and dolling out cash to the first charity that comes knocking or looking for a tax write-off. I mean they are truly involved with charities and they do this by giving their time, money, energy, setting up trusts, and getting involved in events. They really go the distance for a charity they are involved with. Usually it is because they simply want to.

After all, *Time Magazine* selected Bill and Melinda Gates and Bono as People of the Year, not because of their personal accomplishments, but because of their involvement in charities and humanitarian causes. It is because they give and they do it from the bottom of their hearts.

I know some of you might say: "Well, if I had that kind of money, I would be giving to charity too. I would have the time to get involved in charities . . ." Guess what? Many of the most successful people got involved with charities long before they were rich and successful. And just because you are rich and successful does not mean you have a lot of time on your hands. On the contrary, many of the most successful and wealthy people have little or no time for themselves and have to force themselves to make time for the charity that they are involved with.

The power of giving comes from selfless acts where you simply give from your heart. This act of giving is not tied to any special event, holiday, or celebration; it is merely a time when you give from the heart because you want to share what you have and show your appreciation and you give because you truly care. There should not be any other motive behind it. You do not give so that you can get something in return. You give because you *want* to. You do not have to give a lot, any amount is worthy

When you give simply from the heart, you are saying to the universe, your higher power, and your subconscious mind that you truly care and want to share what you have. You are also saying that you do not care if you do not get anything in return; you do not care if no one notices or if no one thanks you.

When you do give in this way, the response that you get can be quite overwhelming. It will be as though a thousand hands come to help you even when you did not ask for help. Things start to fall into place, because those who give from the heart will get back a thousand-fold. Remember, I said that you give from the heart. You do not give with the expectation of getting something in return. You can give with the thought that you are sharing; that you are giving because you have so much.

You are giving because you know and trust that you will always have what you want so you can afford to give something even before you receive what you seek.

This mere act of giving from the heart, with the full knowledge that you have plenty, and with the trust that you will always have more than enough creates a bond between you and your higher power, spirit, universe, subconscious mind, God or whatever you want to call that part of us that we feel is connected to a higher entity. That bond is a trust, in which you are saying, "I know I will always have more than I want so I am now giving something because I want to, fully trusting that I will always have more than what I want and therefore I can share because I want to."

When you do this, the universe, your higher power, and your subconscious mind respond by saying: "Ah-ha, they have so much that they are already willing to share, let us give them some more so that they can continue to share." It really does work that way. You keep getting more because you keep giving.

Too often we get caught up in our wants and needs; we get selfish, focusing only on ourselves and our own little problems which when looked at in terms of the bigger picture are really not that severe.

Sure, there are some of us who have had some serious setbacks that we want to overcome and I am not trivializing that or any of your own personal concerns. However, I do think that we need to look at the needs of those around us as well, and then ask ourselves what we can do to help make things better. After all, it is our world, if we do not share, how can we help each other?

If you do not help your neighbour, who will? There would be no progress because we would all be consumed with our own little worlds and not take the time to help each other. Giving is a part of human nature. That is why when we do it we enjoy the process so much. We enjoy seeing the other person smile; we enjoy helping someone else in some small way.

I know that not all of you are in a position to give a great deal, or to buy the ideal present, or to spend a lot of money. But you can give your time. You can give something small. You can make a small gesture to the universe and your higher power, in the knowledge that you will always have what you want and more. You believe so much that you are willing to give and share this even before you receive it.

The Law of Giving

You may have heard that if you give you will get in return. So you go out and you give, and you give and it seems like you get nothing. Then you say, "This doesn't work" and you stop giving because you are tired and it got you nowhere. Not the way to do it.

What am I talking about?

The law of giving exists. It simply says that if you give you will receive in abundance. The catch to it is that you have to give from your *heart* with no expectations. Sure, you have heard that phrase before, but here is what it means: When you give from your heart, you give with no expectations. You give only because you want to give; because you want to share what you have and because you want to help somebody. I know somebody out there is going to say, "Ah-ha! So I can give to help people and I'll get in return. Great, I'll start giving tomorrow." That is not how it works!

You should never give expecting something in return. Sounds crazy, I know but that is only because we have been conditioned to give so that we get something in return. It is that old "What's in it for me?" approach, which just does not work with the Law of Giving.

Those who are successful, and I mean truly financially successful, such as Paul Newman, Bill Gates, Ted Turner, and Warren Buffett, the list goes on and on, are all involved in charities, many of which they worked with before they were successful.

I know sceptics will say, "Yeah, but for them it's a great tax write-off."

But remember, their time *is not,* and they give from their heart, no strings attached, because they get nothing in return, or at least they do not go in wanting to get something in return. Just so you know, Bill Gates has to date donated close to 2 billion dollars to charities. He and his wife donated a billion this year. Ted Turner is often remembered for the billion dollars that he donated to the UN, but in 1994 he donated 200 million dollars to charities and he has his own non-profit organization fighting for endangered species.

They all donate money and time and they give from the heart.

When you give, and give from the heart, you send out a powerful message that says you are willing to share what you have, and thus the more you have, the more you will share. This is what is picked up by your subconscious mind, the universe, and your higher self. You are then drawn to situations and circumstances that allow you to have more because you will share more. The key is to give from your heart and to give before you receive.

The Importance of Giving

I believe that the act of giving and sharing wealth is one of the key components and responsibilities of being wealthy. There are a variety of reasons why giving is important, and the act itself benefits the giver in countless ways. Here are a few to consider:

Your Legacy

People are remembered not for being rich, but for what they contributed to society while they were alive. Even very rich moguls (Sam Walton, Bill Gates, John Rockefeller, et al) are or will be remembered for how they changed the world, not for their millions or billions. Not all of us can dramatically impact society, but we can all give something back. When you die, no one (save perhaps your heirs) will know or care that you died rich. But you can change someone's life by giving freely your money and your time.

> *"You make a living by what you get;*
> *you make a life by what you give."*
>
> ~Winston Churchill

Your Karma

Giving is a metaphysical act that literally makes you a magnet for whatever you give be it money, love, time, peace, or joy. This may sound like new age mumbo jumbo, but it is seriously true. The more you cling to wealth, just like fame or love, the more it will elude you and the less satisfied you will be with your lot. So if you want to be wealthy, spread the wealth.

> *"There is a wonderful mythical law of nature that the three*
> *things we crave most in life - happiness, freedom,*
> *and peace of mind—are always attained*
> *by giving them to someone else."*
>
> ~Peyton Conway March

175

Your Religion

If you are religious, whether you follow Christianity, Islamism, Judaism or any other religion, you are called to give. Even if you are an atheist or agnostic, the spiritual principle of giving is probably important to you.

CHAPTER 2

MEDITATION

Meditation is a method used to calm the mind and free the body of the stresses of daily living.

How do we meditate?

- Remain still for a moment
- Breathe slowly and release your breath slowly
- Do this several times until the body is relaxed
- Close your eyes and visualise peace, or quiet moments in your life
- Watch your thoughts slowly and see them vanish as the body is relaxed
- Remain quiet and keep a visual image of any peaceful scene
- Repeat in your mind's eye these scenes of peace and quiet
- The end result is a calming feeling throughout the body; you will feel relaxed and peaceful
- Do this for 5 minutes as often as necessary . . .

Deep within us resides an unbelievable piece of machinery that is constantly churning, is never asleep, and keeps our bodies going 24 hours a day. It regulates, it monitors, and, yes, it can be affected by thoughts and beliefs. This is called the superconscious mind. To harness the power of this mind is not difficult, but you must harness it for all the good reasons. It is the sleeping giant, and it could also be very destructive. Suppose you get up one morning and say to yourself, "Today I shall have a great day, nothing less will do." And so you do things that make it a great day, and so the day is concluded on a high note.

The next day, you get up after a bad dream; you are mad at the world and you say to yourself that this is a terrible day. Then everything you do, most likely, will have a negative connotation, and so you do have a bad day.

The sun has risen again, the morning is full of sunshine, and you say to yourself, "I am going to have wonderful days from now on." You do this daily. After a while, your days and thoughts are transformed, and you are a changed person. The very thought commands the superconscious mind to obey instructions, and a new habit is formed. Such is the power of the superconscious mind. I hope you practice this, as it is very effective in moments of meditation.

My friends, this is where I wish to end the topic of religion and the book as well. I have placed all the knowledge and research that I have into this book, and I hope that you have acquired many learnings from this. It is my fervent hope that, as you go on with your lives, you will carry with you the knowledge that you have received through my little nuggets of wisdom.

All that I have written here are thoughts gathered from years of experience. These aspects of life are what I deem to be very important in our search for fulfillment. Whenever we go to sleep, there are moments when we tend to question what we have done during the day, and whether we have received satisfaction. Most of the time, we content ourselves with the thought of that unsure future; of that elusive sense of fulfillment. I hope that, on reading through the pages of this book, you have developed a sense of connection not solely with me, but with your inner self as well.

Do not forget that you are the master and creator of your life. You can change the world if you want to. All you have to do is take that single step towards the improvement of your world and that means starting with yourself; make simple changes and see the difference in your life.

Once we learn to develop and nurture these aspects in our lives, then we are sure to attain that fulfillment, and before we know it, at the end of the day, we'll have a smile on our faces and say, "I have lived a fulfilling day today."

Be the force of change you want to see in the world. Friends, I bid you farewell and the very best!

Copies of this book are available from
the printer of this book.

I wish to give special thanks to all contributors
to this book and to all writers whose quotes
I have used to illustrate my points.